UNLEARNING CREATIVITY

UNLEARNING CREATIVITY

HOW TO UNLEARN THE PARAMETERS OF CREATIVITY WE'VE BEEN CONDITIONED TO

BY SAM BUDIARTHO

NEW DEGREE PRESS

COPYRIGHT © 2020 SAM BUDIARTHO

UNLEARNING CREATIVITY

How to Unlearn the Parameters of Creativity We've Been Conditioned To

ISBN

978-1-64137-973-1   *Paperback*

978-1-64137-853-6   *Kindle Ebook*

978-1-64137-854-3   *Digital Ebook*

This book is for curious inventors of all shapes and sizes.

CONTENTS

———

"We have to continually be jumping off cliffs
and developing our wings on the way down."

—KURT VONNEGUT,
IF THIS ISN'T NICE, WHAT IS? ADVICE FOR THE YOUNG

ACKNOWLEDGMENTS

I've done a lot of crazy things in my life, but writing a book in a year is unparalleled to all else. Words can't describe how grateful I am to be able to savor every crumb of this exploration. It's not every day you wake up to a LinkedIn message from a Georgetown professor asking if you'd like to write a book. I want to first and foremost thank Professor Eric Koester for making this entire experience possible. Without him, none of this could have existed.

Secondly, thank you to my loving parents Rexon & Santhi Budiartho—you both have served to raise and love me unconditionally to the best of your abilities.

I obviously can't thank everyone I've encountered—although I wish I could. My growth is supplied from both the good and the bad experiences I've faced with all the people I have met. So here are a million "thank yous" to everyone I have stumbled across. Fulfilling this dream would not have been possible without each of you.

Along my rocky journey of triumph and fear, I realized that developing *Unlearning Creativity* really takes a village. Thank you to my editors, Jennifer Psujek and Carol McKibben, and alpha readers, Najwa Bou-Melhem and Alexander Baker, who have worked tirelessly to help shape this book.

And finally, thank you to everyone who contributed, big or small, to help me publish my baby, *Unlearning Creativity*.

My eternal thanks to the following people who were interviewed and became a part of this book:

Jeanette (Uber Driver)
Alexander Baker
Nisha Khater
Najwa-Bou Melhem
Timothy Tan
Kiara Tanojo
Corey Bao Nguyen
Derek Garlington

This book would not be possible without the generous support of the following people who pre-ordered, participated as a beta reader, or supported me through my mental breakdowns:

Rexon Budiartho
Santhi Budiartho
Eric Koester
Kelly Peterson
Laura Quirke
Amenda S. Lee
Anaïs Connelly

Sonia Varma
Charlie Andolina
Abdul Azim
Elbert Tiwa
Rafael Wana
Jack Harkin
Ian Leung

Katie DeVries
Kayla Chin
Katherine Wardhana
Arsh Srivastava
Alexandra Anderson
Hendel Charles
Matthew Ong
Riko Morisawa
Natasya Handajuwana
Christopher Walker
Brandon Hulston
Ethan Park
Juan Valderrama
Britney Santoso
Ella Hopp
Nicholas Yuh
Kiara Tanojo
Najwa Bou-Melhem
Alexander Baker
Nisha Khater
Liam Burnstad
Harrison Soegiarto

Helen Smalley
Tarun Titus
Marina Budiman
Rolex Muliawan
Clay Walker Peterson
Jason Bharwani
Clarissa Gunadharma
Robert Yang
Nadia Tendian
Edward R. Tinnemeyer
Alex Fox
Timothy Susanto
Laksh Goyal
Devon Brasali
Vincent Liu
Phoebe Hoang
Fila Oen
Jade Giles
Nicholas Pudjarminta
John Milton
Shane Sullivan

PREFACE

—

I am not the same person I was when writing the introduction of this book. Comparing who I was before this journey started to who I am now feels like stepping into the house you live in, but noticing the wallpaper is different. During the last months of editing, I lost a part of me and felt absent for a while. Those times were not easy. Writing was especially painful. But I've learned that "easy" is the training wheels you were never ready to let go of. Easy doesn't let you ride it out on your own. Easy doesn't let you grow.

INTRODUCTION

UBER RIDES

———

I have a strange endearment for Uber rides. The offbeat stories I've heard from trips with their drivers helped me to realize that creativity is far more than art. It's funny that I only realized the socially defined concept of creativity was flawed once I hit Uber Platinum—which is attained after *a lot* of rides. But life has strange ways of delivering its lessons.

Starting with preschool, students learn the segregation between those who are "creative" and those who are not. The education system fails by labeling only a certain set of students as creative. These students usually excel in traditional art—painting, music, or other art—but not as mathematicians or scientists.

The reality is, though, that everyone is a creative creator, but because society has mated creativity with traditional artists, all others go unrecognized. This epiphany only really hit me when I met Jeanette.

It was mid-October 2019, and it hurt to walk in the rain. It felt as if ants were giving me little kisses. Hardly romantic. I hailed my ride, which was Jeanette driving a white Toyota

Prius. Early on, Jeanette and I introduced ourselves and both happened to be Indonesians living in Los Angeles (though she's also half Kenyan). We engaged in small talk, of course, it was about the weather, about how the rain felt oddly sharp and tingly. As bilinguals, we bonded over the fact that Americans call the sensation "pins and needles" while Bahasa speakers call it *kesemutan*, which translates to ant-ing (the feeling that a million little ants are walking around and biting your skin).

After she took a big gulp of her (what looked like) lemonade, Jeanette delivered a stirring and unexpected monologue: "You know, ants have always fascinated me. Their purpose in life is to follow one another. They scavenge for food and put materials in specific places and form alliances and whatnot. But that's the only thing an ant does. It would be impossible to try and explain to an ant complex scenarios, like how humans enjoy going to escape rooms. Because for some bizarre reason, it's fun to lock yourself in a room and then figure out how to get out."

She made me think about all the fathomless concepts that excite humans; ants will never understand. As insects, they don't have to know these processes to survive.

On the topic of the hierarchy, we started talking about the concept of God, the universe, and other deities. If such things exist, the higher power is beyond our knowledge and perhaps sees us the way we see ants. If we ever try as humans to understand these higher-power beliefs or motivations, we wouldn't be able to know *why* or *how*. It just wouldn't be comprehensible. Similar to trying to think of new colors—it's impossible.

Jeanette questioned these higher-conditioned creatures and if they were even real. We discussed how we'd ever discover their reality.

Right before I left the Uber, Jeanette thanked me for an engaging conversation. She explained that she's an aspiring social worker, who only works for Uber as a side hustle. For the past month, she'd been trying to work on her communication skills for her future job. In every ride, depending on the person, she tried to understand what engages her riders in conversation. She does a little experiment to see what she could say to hold a conversation for the whole ride. I have to admit, the set up was ingenious. A few benefits of this system are that Jeanette:

- Can develop her communication skills through real-life experience with her riders.

- Would meet a lot of personalities, the same way she would as a social worker.

- Is learning without cost. In fact, *she* gets paid to drive around.

- Is set up in an environment where she would not likely see the person again.

  - Since this relationship is understood with both parties, an honest conversation can be carried out.

  - It feels like free therapy. There is no incentive to lie or to be afraid of gossip.

    - And if they do, who cares; you don't know them personally.

Jeanette was the last ride I needed to reach Uber Platinum and an epiphany.

Every other person has a breadth of information and thought processes that vary from yours. Some would rarely cross your mind. It's like listening to an audio book. Except, the stories are rarer, because they cannot be bought from Audible and are not readily accessible to everyone. Similar to books, we might have to agree to disagree with the content. But forming opinions are integral to learning.

While thinking about the dense subject of God and ants, I also found enlightenment in how creative Jeanette was. Creativity is finding unique solutions to problems—no matter the particulars. She was able to find a stable arrangement to efficiently work on her communication skills through Uber. Might I add, it paid off. She really kept me on my toes throughout the ride.

She really made me think about God and philosophical realities on my way to Chipotle.

While eating my carnitas burrito bowl, I thought about the ride a little longer, specifically about the ideas of creativity and knowledge. It's this unexpected connection and transfer of knowledge that makes it exciting to meet new people. It's realizing that these nuances we experience everyday are what allow us to grow our own creative mindsets.

HOW TO BE "CREATIVE"

For years students have been taught "how to be creative," but the harsh reality is creativity cannot be taught. The only way to build the foundation of creativity is to expand our experiences. The concoction of your knowledge is malleable and constantly changing. And that knowledge impacts your creativity, kind of like adding new words into a word bank. You have more to work with. That knowledge can then be broken apart, reinterpreted, and created into new ideas.

As humans, we convert the perception of shapes and colors into meaning all without breaking a sweat. We have trillions of simultaneous connections that allow us to convert sensory perceptions into thoughts, beliefs, and ideas. These ideas may never be thought of by anyone else because of the infinite combinations of our genetic makeup and upbringing. So, how will we know if these ideas are influential if we're reluctant to share them? How will we know what important information someone has without talking to them?

Professor Matthew Lieberman can help us understand a little better. He specializes in social cognitive neuroscience at UCLA. He recently conducted an experiment to search out the intersection of social interaction and the human brain.[1]

Brain size is usually proportional to body size in every animal, except for humans. Human brains are way larger in proportion. For years neurologists have questioned the reasoning behind the disparity in proportion of the human brain. Eager to find an answer, scholars performed some brain scans of individuals doing active tasks such as catching a ball. Though instead of analyzing active tasks, these neurologists

---

1   Emily Smith, "Social Connection Makes a Better Brain," *The Atlantic*, October 29, 2013.

were more interested in what the brain looks like in-between tasks—when we are at complete rest.[2]

Apparently, while the brain is resting, it falls into a configuration feature called the "default network." The main takeaway was that the "default network" looks exactly the same as another configuration feature: social thinking. The reason why our brains are larger in proportion to our bodies, compared to other animals, is because of our enhanced social cognition and thinking.[3]

This means that when our brains are in complete rest, we fall back on thinking about social situations. Specifically in Liberman's words "the default network directs us to think about other people's minds—their thoughts, feelings, and goals."[4]

To explain it further, today you probably let your mind rest for a couple seconds, whether you were lying down in bed after a hot shower, or walking from point A to B. All those times your brain was in complete rest, it was actually actively thinking of social scenarios. After this finding, neurologists started posing another question: Why would the human brain waste energy for thinking socially rather than resting?[5]

Liberman concluded that, "Evolution has made a bet, that the best thing for our brain to do in any spare moment is to get ready for what comes next in social terms."[6]

---

2   Ibid.

3   Ibid.

4   Ibid.

5   Ibid.

6   Ibid.

THE IMPORTANCE OF CONVERSATION

It was only after that Uber ride and coming across Liberman's theory that I realized the importance of conversation, no matter the person. It isn't about specifically engaging with those who are scholars or are notable for whatever reason. It's more about the authentic human experience that all of us go through. It's about the peculiarities of our journeys. Where were you born and what cultural norms did you learn growing up? What has life thrown at you? How did it break your heart or play hard to get with you? Those are stories that I like to collect.

There is something magical about listening to these personal stories and digging deep into what each brain has coalesced.

Maybe they know a theory or fact that you've never even thought could have been possible. Perhaps they know how many ants would weigh the same amount as all the humans on earth. Or something deeper than a weird fact, such as the important lessons they've learned from their mistakes.

Whatever you may learn through another person are the building blocks for creativity. Because of this, schools "teaching" creativity is counterproductive to the development of the actual creative process. Rules box you in the constraints of what you're taught, whether that may be the boundaries of what is art and what isn't or x, y, and z. And I can only tell you now that x, y, and z only facilitate creativity when trying to make words out of mom's alphabet soup.

The Google definition of creativity is: "relating to or involving the use of the imagination or original ideas to create something." This fails to take into account that the imagination that fuels our creativity is built through *experience*. The more we have seen, the more expansive the imagination. We are all walking stocks of information. I'm twenty years of information unique to me. No one else has had, or will ever have, my experience. Not one minute of my entire life is going to be exactly the same as one minute of someone else's life. Knowing this, the stories, experiences, and social connections we find are the nutrients our creativity craves.

When you connect with someone—whether through a passing glance or an intense dinnertime debate—your mind grows and builds a better foundation for creativity. Thus, there is a strong relationship between the people we meet and creativity.

A LESSON REINFORCED
The world has put in a great amount of effort to teach me that lesson.

Later, in February 2020, the sun cascaded down the buildings of downtown Los Angeles. All the muddy puddles on the pavement glistened. It was a pretty day, to say the least. A great day to continue writing my introduction for this book at an outdoor café. After calling my Uber, I was too distracted by the sun to realize that it was Jeanette in a white Toyota Prius.

No, it can't be.

With the size of Los Angeles and the thousands of Uber drivers, it can't be the *same* Jeanette. It can't be the Uber driver that I have been writing my introduction about. We couldn't have been in the same location at the same time, four months later.

But it *was* the same Jeanette. I swear on my favorite toe.

For the first couple minutes of our ride, we caught each other up on what happened within our lives since we last spoke, like old friends do. I asked her if she got the social worker position. She took a big gulp of (I'm suspecting again) her lemonade, smiled, and said, "Yes I did, but I turned it down. Two weeks ago, when I was testing my conversational skills, I had a rider who looked like a professional man. Sleek hair with thick dark sunglasses. You know, one of those heavy looking kinds, not the cheap ones from *H&M* that break easily. So I decided to talk to him about all these marketing ideas I had... and he really just asked me to visit his office for an interview. Now I'm a campaign manager. It's almost quadruple the pay of the social worker position, and I start next month."

Meeting Jeanette for the second time made me think a lot about chance. The chances of stumbling upon that job offer were slim to none. The chance of re-meeting Jeanette was also slim to none. How serendipitous. If that isn't a life lesson to talk to everyone you meet, in any setting, I don't know what is. These chances are slim to begin with, so why not create an environment that increases these occurrences?

Without Jeanette talking to her rider, she wouldn't have been recruited.

Without me talking to Jeanette, who knows how different this introduction would have been? I can only wonder if this book would've had the same bones and meat, or if it would've existed in the same way at all.

Before our ride ended, I told her that I'd actually been writing about her. Here, in this book. That I was writing about social connection and creativity, and that she was my opening story. My introduction. I didn't think I would have met her again to be able to tell her that. Against all odds, I met her again by chance while editing the story.

Again, life has its strange ways of delivering lessons.

Now I'm here writing the lessons given to me to pass on. To show you that cuddling up to social connections has its perks in providing you rich lessons—that human connection, knowledge, and creativity are concepts that are all inherently intertwined.

WHAT THIS BOOK MIGHT MEAN TO YOU

You'll have the opportunity to take away knowledge from this book and be able to manipulate it into your own understanding. I've always had the privilege to believe that I am creative because the work I produce coincides with socially defined concepts. I just happen to be a two-dimensional visual artist, who fuels creativity through charcoal powder instead of numbers. What you can expect to find as you read here is the idea that *everyone* is creative, and that everyone should have that privilege to believe so. Even if your kindergarten teacher told your parents you weren't artistically gifted.

It'll be clearer to understand that there is art and creativity involved in solving math equations and analyzing data. Too often we are taught to think outside the box, but within a larger bubble. Truthfully, creativity cannot be confined to either of these constraints—what exists and what doesn't is up to the creator. You'll see how humans connect and learn, and thus produce creative work in diverse mediums.

I started writing this book because there's nothing that means more to me than social connection and creativity. I feel responsible to contribute to a paradigm shift in making others believe that creativity is more than just traditional art. Throughout the chapters I showcase interviews with many different creators—from a screenwriter to a computer science major—to demonstrate that creativity exists everywhere.

Besides being from diverse career paths, the interviewees are also from varied cultural backgrounds. I myself approach this process after growing up in international schools and having moved from Singapore to Indonesia to (currently) America for college. This background has allowed me the privilege to meet so many unique individuals with such contrasting backgrounds. These differences in the way we grow are important in how they shape our understanding, perspectives, and creative process—so I made it a goal to showcase a diverse array of people.

I hope my writing will open the eyes of creators, artists, pop psychologists, and especially those who don't believe that what they do is creative. Creativity does not exclude analytical individuals that may not follow the career path of traditional art. This book is also meant for those who want to actively unlearn stringent creativities or thinking processes—to redefine creative work, and to learn on your own terms.

Finally, I also hope that after reading this, readers will realize the importance of social connection—encouraging you to seek new conversations with anyone. A stranger walking down the street, your professor, or someone you're in the elevator with. You never know what they know that might expand your own worldview.

We are all creators who use creativity in different fields for varied solutions. It could be designing a sustainable power plant, or finding ways to wake up early on a rainy Sunday morning (because you currently have an affair with the Snooze Button instead of staying loyal to Getting Up). Big or small, to survive, we all become creators.

1

PEOPLE WATCHING & LEARNING (FAKE) CREATIVITY

Orange Juice & Bruises

you look in the mirror
    purple
        swollen
            tender
you reach for the bottom left cabinet
and it creaks louder than yesterday
the hollow space carries nothing besides your
    bundle of remedies
consisting of Band Aids and color-correcting
    concealer
but you're already prepared for the makeup to
    smudge later in the day,
for the bruise to peek through each follicle of
    powder

but you don't know why,
you keep falling into the same routine
of letting them give you another
and another
and
another

~

you pour your orange juice
right after brushing your teeth,
but you're already prepared for the bitterness,
because at this point you're
          indifferent
                    numb
                              nonchalant
you know that toothpaste is a surfactant,
that suppresses your sweet tongue receptors;
the sulfate in the toothpaste breaks
    down phospholipids,
increasing bitterness
but you don't know why,
you keep falling into the same routine
of drinking orange juice
right after toothpaste devours your receptors
you allow bitterness
to overcome sweetness
every single
morning

~

you slip in your earbuds
and queue their least favorite song
because it's your "favorite"
you turn up the volume,
the loudest it goes
and you tell yourself you feel
 content
  happy
   free
but you already know that's a lie
you trick yourself into thinking they're not on
 your mind anymore
but really
you've just become a master at transforming them
 into metaphors.

—Sam Budiartho

The days you don't want to write are the days you should write. It trains the mind to be on its toes and full of productive creativity. You write from a different perspective, tone, and angle when you don't want to write. Sometimes that perspective can be beautiful.

Before I developed this poem, I wrote (from start to finish) a twelve-page comparison of two sculptures—the Head of Iris and one from Ptolemaic Egypt. A full day of constricting MLA-format writing. It's strange because I think this is one of the better poems I've written. Or maybe it's better because it was born on a day of otherwise utter dryness. Whatever it may be, I was able to carve a poem out of the simple concept of shoving things under the rug—metaphorically and physically.

We shy away from our feelings, our realities, and disguise them with metaphors to make them more palatable and more poetic.

On days where I am unmotivated to write, I tell myself false realities—that I can't write because I'm uninspired, I can't write because I've already written a lengthy college essay and I've burnt myself out. But writing is writing. Being able to convert thoughts to the material world with paper and pen, or keyboard and screen is always doable. We often shy away from these realities and fold them into excuses.

Writing this poem helped me unpack those thoughts, and all the other metaphors I've written into my own life. It made me feel more creative, to be able to drag something worthy from a place of staleness. After striking my flint what seemed like a hundred times, my tinder finally caught fire—even though my mind was not there.

I began to wonder what is implied when feeling creative. I began to wonder about creativity—its facets and definitions.

What does it *mean* to be creative?

THE SEARCH FOR CREATIVITY: MY IMAGINARY COUCH SOLOMON

In my daily quest to seek inspiration, I watch how creativity is carried out by others, through an imaginary couch. Growing up, I was that kid that had an imaginary friend until pretty late in my life. Over the years as a tribute to this friend, Solomon, I began transferring all his characteristics into a couch.

I only started referring to Solomon as a couch when I turned nine; my Dad had recently bought me an *Introduction to Psychology* book for my birthday.

Solomon was a stolen idea from the book, specifically from Sigmund Freud, the founding father of psychoanalysis. Freud first came up with the idea to help unwind both the patient and the analyst in the nineteenth century. This idea of the "psychoanalyst's couch" became popular and appeared in many American movies as early as the 1930s.[7]

Today, no one really lies down on a couch in therapy, since there is no empirical evidence that this method is more effective than sitting in a chair. Now, the couch exists merely as a symbol of Freudian psychoanalysis.

For me, Solomon is a symbol of how I people-watch and gather their ways of implementing creativity. I take him everywhere I go, psychoanalyzing all who inhabit his reach. My subjects are oblivious to my slight obsession with decoding their mannerisms. In the adventures that Solomon and I have, I realized that I've always been interested in how individuals curate creative solutions toward their problems.

An Asian couple in a food court unintentionally warmed up Solomon as my first visitors. Holding hands, they looked like they were in love. Gazing into each other's eyes, they looked as if no one could understand *this* love, *their* love. It was something intimate they shared, even though the feeling

---

7   Susannah Stevens, "How this couch changed everything," *BBC*, June 18, 2015.

has already been described in a thousand songs, movies, and books.

As they gazed over their steamed dumplings, I began examining each of their hands. They were both holding chopsticks, using the top stick like a pencil while pressing the other with their ring fingers. Watching closely, I wrapped my little fingers around my own two wooden sticks and slowly learned the complicated mechanics of chopsticks—while questioning what love meant.

After that lunch, I was hooked on the distant observation of people on my couch. Little did I know, it would become my favorite pastime. My analyses of different behaviors has consistently provided unexpected but critical life lessons. Even something as simple as the use of chopsticks is critical; any ounce of knowledge is essential to creativity.

After a few years, my continued use of Solomon caused his leather finish to become faded and distressed. I was that annoying twelve-year-old that asked too many questions—but those answers were sitting on Solomon, waiting to be analyzed.

To give a couple examples of my adventures with Solomon, I'll paint a picture of the day we went to splurge on food. This was in a small restaurant that my parents loved to take me on Sundays after church. My lunch would start off with guacamole, but the real appetizer was sitting in a booth across from me—a sleepy woman taking Melatonin supplements.

Is sleep basically time-traveling into the future?

Instead of devouring my entree of Nasi Padang, I watched a man enter the restaurant and considered the possibilities of why he could be staring at the menu for so long.

Is that the restaurant's fault because the layout is too rigid, or is he just indecisive?

When the Mochi came, Solomon was occupied by a girl with the Ursa Major asterism tattooed across her shoulder blades.

Are all constellations brought upon by the jealousy of Hera and Zeus?

All these questions, in a way, helped fuel my inspiration; puzzlement is often the first step of learning and creativity. All who tenanted Solomon were influential, no matter their gravity, but the visitor who altered my artistic vision the most was the Tuxedo Man.

I was fourteen and old enough to "enjoy" a—gross and bitter—cup of coffee. I couldn't mind my own business and focus on my essay regarding imperialism, so I decided to take a break. This led to watching the Tuxedo Man, seated conveniently beside me at the café. He pulled out his Mont Blanc pen and began sketching obscure animals on the paper table cloth. It seemed like something that was fueled by spontaneity. He didn't draw a grid to figure out proportions, he just drew. It clearly didn't matter how lopsided or disproportionate his figures were so long as his pen kept moving to the pace and flow of his imagination.

Watching him, I began drawing half-octopus, half-shark creatures—with my own touch. I started to research the bone structure of these creatures on my phone. I decided, in this new style, I wanted to keep a balanced level of what was real and what was imagined, mainly to confuse viewers. To grasp their attention longer.

It was the first time I drew something that had no solid rules, finally in open rebellion against the artistic confinements I had put on myself. In previous drawings, I'd stick to arrangements that "made sense." Things that existed—birds that look like the letter "m" in the distance, the sun in the corner of the page. Cliché-infused ideas.

After analyzing Tuxedo Man, I decided to create an iPhone case line called Exfoli. I hand drew surrealistic images of animals, humans, and flowers and printed them on cases. I co-founded Exfoli in high school. The reason behind the invention was purely just as a personal passion project. Starting Exfoli as a small Instagram business at fifteen wouldn't have happened without Tuxedo Man, but especially without Solomon.

I am always looking for the next individual to inspire, infuriate, or entertain me. Solomon is the medium for that transfer of knowledge. With him, I look toward others, thinking about the creative solutions they've used personally, which in turn helps foster my own creative endeavors. If I had to pinpoint what started my passion for psychology and creating art, it would have to be Solomon. Or I guess, my dad, for the psychology book.

When you've thought of an ingenious idea, it's vital to trace the origin of that thought. When was that seed planted? Was it while you were cooking with thyme, or maybe while taking the hottest shower to date? After thinking about the seed, it's also essential to think about what acted as the water. What actions helped you along the way to bring that ingenious idea into the material world?

Solomon is a mechanism that leads me to my creative process. I consider him to be the start of almost all my creative works. Developing my own tool helped me navigate my relationship with art. We all have our own devices to fuel our creativity. Even if it's not an invisible couch—any form is always valid.

DEFINING CREATIVITY:
SIR KEN ROBINSON & DR. TIM LEUNIG

The idea of creativity has always been defined, contested, and redefined by many scholars. There, however, are two growing perspectives: one by educationalist Sir Ken Robinson and another by economist Tim Leunig. These perspectives go neck to neck, and are opposites of each other.

According to the About the Author page of Sir Ken Robinson's book, *Out of Our Minds: Learning to be Creative*, "In 2005 he was named as one of Time/Fortune/CNN's Principle Voices. In 2003, he received a knighthood from Queen Elizabeth II for his services to the arts."[8]

It is clear he has always had a strong passion for advocating a creativity-friendly environment in schools. Sir Ken Robinson

---

8   Ken Robinson, *Out of Our Minds: Learning to be Creative* (Mankato: Capstone, 2017), xxi.

explains in a TED talk that "we don't grow into creativity, we grow out of it. Or rather, we get educated out of it."[9] He argues that creativity is a direct by-product of our imaginations.

Students are punished when making a mistake; we've grown up expecting that our education must be carefully mapped out to reach success. A lot of students fall into the trap of memorizing answers or finding shortcuts in information retention to get good grades. These grades allow them to get into a great college, and then a great job. It's a transactional relationship between going to school and a stable income. Robinson takes this paradigm and questions: What happens to our creativity during this all too familiar journey?

Robinson believes that "our education system has mined our minds in the way we strip mine the earth for a particular commodity."[10] What he is referring to here is that schools have trained the mind to be great at test taking and memorization, but rarely for fostering the growth of innovative thinking and creativity. We're taught to measure our creativity by how well we can draw perfect figures and color within the lines.

Dr. Tim Leunig argues the opposite. In his TED talk, Leunig introduces himself as "the chief analyst and chief scientific advisor at the English department of Education," and he is also a professor at the London School of Economics.[11] Leunig

9   Ken Robinson, "Do schools kill creativity?" filmed February 2006 in Monterey, CA, TED video, 6:28.

10 Ken Robinson, "Do schools kill creativity?" filmed February 2006 in Monterey, CA, TED video, 18:14.

11 *TED*, "Tim Leunig: Why real creativity is based on knowledge," October 17, 2016, video, 0:22.

explains that innovative ideas that have been created since the Industrial Revolution until today are solely based on knowledge from education.[12] His stance is that we don't grow out of creativity in schools, instead we build a foundation for that creativity.

Leunig says, regarding Ken Robinson, that "he is flat wrong to claim that schools are killing creativity," instead that "real creativity is based on knowledge."[13]

I don't completely agree with Leunig's first statement, but definitely agree with this second. There is some sense in Robinson's argument that schools are hindering creativity. But there are a growing number of schools that work harder on encouraging their students to *understand* the material instead of memorize and are thus able to foster creativity. Those schools ask the "why" questions on tests that require judgement and knowledge, rather than a photographic memory.

The argument that I am creating throughout this book situates itself between these two perspectives. Creativity is built upon both knowledge and our imagination; it is the relationship, tension, and play between the two. Without knowledge, the basis for creativity is limited. On the other hand, without imagination, the barriers of reality block our creative flow.

The knowledge we learn and experience can in turn be leveraged to fuel creative thinking. But, if we always ground

---

12   *TED,* "Tim Leunig: Why real creativity is based on knowledge," October 17, 2016, video, 2:35.

13   *TED,* "Tim Leunig: Why real creativity is based on knowledge," October 17, 2016, video, 5:50.

ourselves in realistic terms, we could never grasp future possibilities. We would be stuck thinking about the same comfortable and mundane ideas.

WHO IS CREATIVE: QWERTY

Since the education system decides who deserves to be creative, we grow up believing that the label "creative" is reserved for traditional artists.

Something that we use every day that you wouldn't have initially thought involved creativity is the making of the QWERTY arrangement on your keyboard.

Many individuals grow up as creative people who don't believe they deserve the title. They simply don't recognize their creativity. Too often we hear, "I'm not a creative person. I'm better at math and science," because we often overlook that math and science are non-traditionally conforming arts that also involve creativity, in their own right.

Christopher Sholes, the inventor of the QWERTY typewriter, was a creative individual. He invented the revolutionary arrangement as we all know it now in 1868, and it continues to be used to this day. Before the QWERTY version, the keyboard had two rows with the keys ordered alphabetically.[14] On the surface level, it made sense—users wouldn't have to search for specific keys since it was arranged in an order they were familiar with.

---

14   Harald Sack, "Christopher Latham Sholes invented the QWERTY Typewriter," *SciHi Blog,* February 14, 2018.

It didn't work out.

The metal arms of the typewriter would collide too often—typically when the typist pressed keys near each other around the same time. Sholes realized that the jams could be reduced through increasing the time it takes for the typist to press one letter after another. He had to figure out common two-letter combinations to separate the keys. So Sholes and his partners conducted a frequency study of letter-pairs in the English language and iterated the keyboard structure many times to separate these pairs equally. Finally, the last iteration was QWERTY.[15]

Why do we still use QWERTY even on devices that aren't a mechanical keyboard? Because introducing a paradigm shift of another arrangement is ambitious after decades of QWERTY acclimation. There's no reason to change it up anyway.

Sholes didn't paint a picture or write a poem, but he still used creativity through iteration to find a unique solution. True and effective iteration is central to creativity. It enables the creator to ask new questions, which facilitate a journey to remarkable discoveries.

Here, both Tim Leunig and Sir Ken Robinson's theory of creativity is implemented. Leunig's theory is seen through the research Sholes and his partners did. Without backbone research and knowledge of how a mechanical typewriter works, Sholes wouldn't have been able to find a plausible solution.

---

15   Ibid.

In Robinson's perspective, without imagination and thinking outside of the traditional order of the English alphabet, future iterations would have been harder to develop to reach QWERTY. Reading the thought process of Sholes, you might think: "That makes sense; I would've done the same to solve that problem."

Chances are, you only think that way because you've been aided with the process of the solution. In the absence of the idea to separate our regular alphabetical order, could you imagine how long it would've taken you to think of that solution? To change something so ingrained in society such as the order of the alphabet?

Everyone has their own relationship with creativity, even if it isn't traditionally conforming.

After years of believing that only traditional artists deserve the label of creative, it's hard to move away from that definition, especially when applied to yourself. That's the box that we, as learners, have unfortunately been confined to or outside of.

LEARNING FALSE CREATIVITY: DEAR MRS. AKIRA

A personal example of Robinson's argument that schools harm our creative mindset from my own past is Mrs. Akira's Kindergarten-2 class. It was the first time I was taught "how to be creative." I only remember because, from that moment forward, I disliked drawing. Thankfully, over the years, I found the path back to my passion. Now, whenever my parents curate my sketches, my mom always asks me why I refused to draw when I was younger. What changed?

Here's the answer you've been waiting for, Mom.

The room was cold, small, and lit with those annoying bright fluorescent lights. The walls were covered in chalky black-boards and multiplication table posters. Yes, posters, plural. There were four, to make sure all the students could see one from every angle of the room. Luckily, if you stood between Mrs. Akira's desk and her potted plants, you couldn't see any of the posters—that's where I mostly sat. That's also probably why I get anxious during job interviews that require mental math.

Richard, my best friend at the time, also sat there, and still doesn't have his multiplication tables memorized (I even gave him a little call the other day to make sure of it). We were both "bad" students: we weren't great at English reading comprehension, math, or Mandarin. We were both more driven to draw instead of solving equations.

We had just moved up to Kindergarten-2, and all the teachers made it a priority to "teach" us creativity, how to be creative, and how to "do art." Ms. Akira passed around thin sheets of paper and a bunch of markers in all the colors we could think of. We were a little too excited about this, since we were previously only allowed to write with black or dark blue ink.

Richard and I looked at each other, both enthralled and con-fused. We started passing each other notes, marked with our scribbled handwriting, guessing what our colorful pens would be used for. Turns out, Ms. Akira wanted us to use proportions to draw similar replicas of different fruits.

We were in kindergarten.

But then again, we were in Singapore. Singapore's education system is one of the best, with most students scoring extremely high on international standardized tests—ask anyone who has grown up through the system, and they will surely confirm the rigorous standards. The heavy use of memorization and obsession with grades starts at a very young age. The strict systems and linear paths to learning also start at a very young age.

Since this was our first introduction to creativity as impressionable children, it was such an important time that should've allowed us to explore all our personal definitions of creativity and what art meant to each of us individually.

But by confining us to strict rules from the get go, Mrs. Akira enforced the exact message that Robinson discussed. She was stifling the very foundations of our creativity. Though as impressionable children, we didn't know that these were life-long lessons that would inevitably mold our definition of creativity. We just did as we were told and focused on drawing proportionate apples.

Ms. Akira placed apples on our desks and told us to draw them the best we could, to translate what we saw onto paper. Naturally, as kindergarteners and humans, some kids were better than others. Some more talented in the domain of a steady hand.

This doesn't mean that that person was more creative than the rest, but we were taught to think that way, starting from age seven. Sitting in our individual tables and looking straight at the chalkboard, examples were taped up. Examples of what the perfect apple drawings looked like.

What was interesting to see was the way we were graded. Our grades were based on how similar our drawn apples looked compared to the actual apples. Usually, kindergarten art classes are graded based on effort. But no, we were deducted points every time we colored outside the apples or if we had a lopsided potato-looking shape. Even then it didn't make sense to me that our artistic creations were encouraged from a linear methodology.

If they told us to simply draw an apple without additional rules, a lot more artists would've been born in that classroom. Not because they'd teach us how to be artists, but because we'd be more inclined to explore—to believe that we were creative in different mediums. Imagine if one of those kids preferred abstract art, but was forced to create quite the realistic opposite. This class defined hyperrealism as the only form of drawing. This was their way of defining what art was for us: proportionate apples.

There are more ways to draw an apple than to replicate an actual apple; there are countless other interpretations and representations. When focusing on drawing in this way at such a young age, Robinson's conclusion is right—we were educated out of creativity. The result dulled our motivation to find solutions that break the norm.

I'm lucky to have had other classes, as I grew older, that fostered creativity. Finally, the prompts given were too large for any two answers to be the same. That's when creativity is sparked. The exact process of finding the solution is not given, or asked to be replicated.

Of course, there is value and beauty in learning the techniques of hyper-realistic art—they help refine the beautiful things you create. But technique alone is not enough, and it shouldn't have been our sole and overriding introduction to creativity.

Again, creativity cannot be taught; it can only be fostered. It is an innate quality in all that can only be built upon through trial and error. With iterations. Remember the first time you created something truly yours, and how you came back for seconds, thirds, and fourths? It is empowering to create something unique. Whether that is developing a new recipe or the process of taking a unique photograph.

Most of the time, our thoughts are confined in this box of what "creativity is," even when we don't know it. Subconsciously, we've been put into these boxes of what's right and what's wrong where there is no space for imperfection and bending the rules.

Just when I thought I couldn't be an even worse student, I became one of those kids who was often sent to the corner of shame. Once art class was implemented into our curriculum, the head of school would have to call my mom regularly to tell her to pick me up because I wouldn't stop crying.

I know you remember, Mom, sorry for the stress I caused you.

Every time I walked into that classroom, with Mrs. Akira telling me how to create art, a screaming tantrum would burst out of me. Because even my seven-year-old self knew there are no rights or wrongs with art, so how can you physically teach and work within these boundaries?

For a while, I felt ashamed whenever I drew something that didn't fit in her itty bitty constraints. I didn't think I'd ever grow to be an artist. Now though, I feel like my seven-year-old self would be both proud and shocked with how far I've come. Today, I know I have the capabilities to draw a proportionate hyper-realistic apple. I've just never tried to.

I wonder why.

Mrs. Akira did discourage me from doing a lot of things—doodling, using the fat brush, glitter—and would force me to follow the specific guidelines she had built for me, which she claimed, would make me a better artist. She was always obviously insinuating to think outside the box, but inside the bigger box of her classroom.

If by some cosmic coincidence she's reading this, then,

Dear Mrs. Akira,

No, I don't want to draw the perfect still life. I don't want to be in a class where all twenty-four of the students are producing replicas of each other's work. I want to draw that aggravating feeling of sand stuck between sweaty toes, or awe from a warm breeze in the spring. Illustrating these sensations are hard. Too often art is viewed as something that "looks nice," but rarely as something that makes me feel—but that's why I keep trying and exploring. You made me realize that there's so much more to art than just making the canvas look pretty and neat. That's all you spoke about, the aesthetics of the page and the proportions of the piece. But it's far more than that. Between your class and today, I've learned that:

- *Developing an environment for creativity is an essential tool, especially when you aren't in the mood for it.*

  - *I always want to break away from the false realities I've invented for myself.*

- *Everyone has a unique creative process for discovering solutions, even if they don't realize it.*

  - *Mine began with my imaginary couch, Solomon.*

- *Creativity is the intersection between imagination and knowledge.*

  - *Ken Robinson conveys the idea that innate imagination is needed to think of innovative solutions. When one hundred percent grounded in reality, it's hard to find new solutions.*

    - *Dreaming big is essential; shatter the constraints that traditional education often places.*

  - *From Tim Leunig's perspective, education is important because knowledge is foundational to enacting creativity.*

- *Knowledge helps us know what's out there as a basis to work with and build off of.*

- *Traditional and non-traditional art use an equal amount of creativity.*

  - *Even though the socially defined concept of creativity states otherwise.*

2

YOUR TRIPLE THREAT: CREATIVITY, EMPATHY, & LOGIC

SOLVING GRANDMA'S HOUSE:
REFLECTION ON OUR CREATIVE PROCESSES

The walls were covered with a vintage rose pattern that had a peculiarly familiar coral wash. Alex and I were stuck in a narrow room, a botanically printed armchair to the side and a lonely shelf on the wall above. In front of the chair rested a pair of freakishly slender antennas growing out of an old CRT television. In the corner room, there was a small but cozy kitchen with an oddly rounded eggshell-white refrigerator. The lady on an overhead speaker signaled that we had seventy minutes to complete the challenge: a grandma-themed escape room.

Although it was intriguing to figure out how to escape, I was watching Alex most of the time. As a self-named psychoanalyst, I wanted to see him mesh his prior knowledge with the given clues to create a solution. This time the subject of my dear couch Solomon was solely Alex; he definitely warmed up the couch.

To explain the context further, Alex Baker was born in the city of Corpus Christi, Texas. I knew of Alex Baker when he moved to Indonesia, during our high school years. He was in the year ahead of me, and our only interaction was sitting in the same room every Monday for a National Honor Society club meeting. We never spoke to each other, minded our own business. Years carried on like that until I left home for college, and ended up attending the same college as Alex.

It's strange to be attending university in the same country—let alone the same college—after going to high school together in a completely different region of the world. Just like the strange Uber driver encounter, life has an interesting take on delivering valuable people into your life.

The first time we formally introduced ourselves in Los Angeles, it was enlightening to see how different we processed and reflected upon information. Alex is a computer science major and started coding because he said that that discipline "meshes with [his] natural way of thinking. The way that you have to think about coding is the same way that [he] thinks in general." It occurred to me that computer science majors are always seen as logical, but rarely as creative.

So I made it a small observational experiment to defy this assumption. This way, I was able to see Alex's physical manifestation of thinking and compare it with my utterly different process; to show that there is no right or wrong way, just *different* ways.

The set up was perfect because debunking Grandma's room directly engaged our creative processes.

We began rummaging around the place to find something, anything to serve as a clue—looking at the objects as if they were intentional glowing beacons we had to investigate.

For those of you who are unfamiliar with escape rooms, the easiest way to solve one is to go as a group—but to choose very, very different people, who work well together, to form that group. Diverse perspectives directly allow for more ideas. When I say different perspectives, I mean both mentally and physically.

Being five foot two, I was too short to see the square holders placed on the top shelf of the room. Thankfully Alex was there to let me know that the four squares were required to be filled—with what? We were unsure at that point.

Two puzzles in Grandma's room are essential in order to illustrate the differences between how Alex and I think. The first puzzle was a numbers problem. Behind the CRT television, a generator required the correct combination of batteries to match the number of watts needed. At this point, sweating from the time crunch, I wished I had sat directly in front of a multiplication times table poster in Mrs. Akira's classroom.

Maybe it would've prepared me for this day.

As I was internally freaking out, not knowing where to begin in solving the problem, Alex was already on it. He tried out different battery combinations to see what worked and what didn't. He took a mental note of which batteries he used, and which combinations he hadn't tried out so far, and thought it through in logical order to avoid forgetting.

With hindsight it seems obvious, but at the time I was unable to think of the easiest way to solve that problem. Personally, as a "right-brain dominant," the thought process didn't immediately click with me in the moment. But since Alex is often labeled as a "left-brain dominant," it made complete sense to him. He could work it out calmly.

LEFT & RIGHT BRAIN FUNCTIONS OR JUST ANALYTICAL & VISUAL THINKING?

A *Psychology Today* article titled, "Are you Left-or Right-Brain Dominant?" explains that left-brain dominant individuals (such as Alex) "are more likely to be clinical and cold in their judgments and problem-solving. Language recognition is a function of the left hemisphere, too, and that makes languages easier for those with left-brain dominance."[16] This explanation of the left-brain could also be the reason why Alex excels in computer science. Since left-brained individuals are better at learning languages, they also tend to catch on faster with learning code.

On the opposite side of the spectrum, right-brain dominance (like mine) "is associated with creativity, emotion, and intuition [...] Right-brain dominant people are characterized as

---

16   E.E. Smith, "Are You Left- or Right-Brain Dominant?" *Psychology Today*, October 19, 2012.

artistic, [...] and often random. Their thought processes are sometimes viewed as irregular and roundabout."[17]

But, it is essential to understand that these segregations are often misunderstood. You are not *either* left or right-brained, but a combination of *both*. Some people may not have a hemisphere dominance, while others may be inclined to one side. Even then, both hemispheres work together.

For example, regarding his work Alex explains that "even though coding is just a sequence of letters and numbers, it's still a product of somebody's thinking and creating something unique. So, taking a new type of problem and trying to come up with a solution is definitely a creative process, no matter what medium you're working through." The left and right brain are in coordination—while coding involves analytical thinking, an attribute of the left brain, it also requires creativity, a characteristic of the right.

The second important puzzle in Grandma's room was based on visual design. In the kitchen, next to the white refrigerator, there was a square carved out from the wooden table top. Scattered around the room were different shaped blocks that were meant to be placed correctly in the square. After we gathered all the pieces, we realized there were more blocks than needed to complete the square puzzle—a tactic to throw us off.

This time, I was the one quick to act. I laid out all the blocks we had in front of me and started visualizing different combinations that would fit together. In my head, I was able to

---

17   Ibid.

flip and rotate the blocks to think of possible solutions and started physically putting them together. It's easier for me to arrange my thoughts visually, rather than to think it through programmatically. The solution came to me what felt like randomly. It was as though I could picture the pieces joined in my head and my hands followed suit.

Even though Alex demonstrates left-brain traits and I seem to be right-brain dominant, there has been some ongoing debate about the idea of dominance. Is there really such a harsh segregation between the two hemispheres? Can you even be completely one-sided?

In 2017, Robert H. Shmerling, published an article titled "Right Brain/Left Brain, Right?" on the Harvard Health Blog (the article was then updated in 2019). Shmerling is an Associate Professor of Medicine at Harvard Medical School and posted this article in hopes to illustrate the debate around brain dominance.[18]

In the introduction of the article, Shmerling states that "according to conventional wisdom, people tend to have a personality, thinking style, or way of doing things that is either right-brained or left-brained." He also goes on to explain that right-brained individuals are deemed to be "intuitive and free thinkers," while left-brainers are "more qualitative and analytical."[19]

But this segregation may be false. Shmerling goes to show that there are some brain functions that rely on one side of

---

18   Robert H. Shmerling, "Right brain/left brain, right?" Harvard Health Publishing, August 25, 2017, updated November 8, 2019.

19   Ibid.

the brain more than the other, explaining that "we know this in part from what is lost when a stroke affects a particular part of the brain."[20]

Although, according to the health professor, if doctors performed an MRI scan of a "mathematician and compared it to the brain of an artist, its's unlikely you'd find much difference."[21] This finding became the turning point for brain dominance discourses.

Even though Shmerling found evidence that suggested brain dominance isn't necessarily overriding, he goes on to conclude the article by asking and answering: "Is the idea of thinking with the left side of your brain a myth? Maybe. But, the lack of proof does not prove the opposite. For people living thousands of years ago, an inability to prove the earth was round did not prove the earth was flat!"[22]

Since scientists haven't come out with definitive answers, throughout this chapter the left and right brain commentary can be thought of as interchangeable with analytical and visual thinking—depending on what future research points to as the truth about brain dominance.

SCHEMA: OUR PERSONAL MENTAL STRUCTURES

After escaping the room, an employee told us that most people get stuck on those two specific puzzles (the generator and

---

20 Ibid.

21 Ibid.

22 Ibid.

the square visual problem). On average, others take longer to solve them.

However, it wasn't only our innate brain/thinking dominance that allowed us to solve these puzzles quickly. What else can help support problem solving?

The schemas we develop for ourselves.

Sir Frederic Bartlett is a British psychologist that developed the foundation of schema theory in 1932. Bartlett's theory suggests that our understanding of the world is formed by a network of abstract mental structures: schemas. We use these imagined structures to understand a literal form of something. It shows the knowledge we've acquired is readily available to be applied in our everyday lives.[23]

Schemas are useful because they allow us to take shortcuts in interpreting the vast amount of information available in our environment. As experiences happen and new information is presented, new schemas are developed and old schemas modified.[24] Even under rapidly changing conditions, humans don't usually have to spend a great deal of time interpreting things. Since schemas are the frameworks we've made for each scenario and situation based on past experience, people can assimilate this new information quickly and automatically from the guidelines.

---

23 Claus-Christian Carbon and Sabine Albrecht, "Bartlett's Schema Theory: The Unreplicated 'Portrait d'homme' Series from 1932," *Quarterly Journal of Experimental Psychology* 65, no. 11 (November 2012): 2258–70.

24 Ibid.

In a way, schemas track our knowledge. An easy example that my high school teacher used to exemplify a schema is the horse-cow distinction. A young child may first develop a schema for a horse. She knows that a horse is large, has hair, four legs, and a tail. These attributes become the structure of her schema for a horse, so when the little girl sees a cow for the first time, she might initially call it a horse.

Only after she sees more cows and horses to refine her schema will she know how to differentiate between these two animals.

Going back to the two puzzles in Grandma's escape room, the reason why Alex and I were quicker than the others in solving the two problems is because of differences in our past experiences, and thus, schemas.

Alex's schema for number analysis is more robust and structured than mine, simply because he has dealt with this thinking more than I have throughout his computer science career. In the same way, I have a more elaborated version of the schema used for visual analysis, simply because I draw and expose myself to the visual arts more.

DEEP DIVE INTO ALEX BAKER: LOGIC & CREATIVITY
When I asked Alex how he sees the world, I was surprised to hear his answer:

"I see the world as a collection of random events that have no particular importance or significance. Everything is based on either the luck of your genetics, where you were born, meeting certain people, or situations that you find yourself in. It's just a cosmic coincidence that everyone is born in a certain place, to a certain family, and because of that, lives and acts a certain way. We're all just floating around in a structure with no real order. It's just kind of a free-for-all."

When I asked him if he thinks coding is creative, he said, "A lot of coding is using previous knowledge to put your thoughts into a physical code, telling the computer what you want it to do. That's creative because, like all art, it's something that you have thought about in a way that nobody else has."

Listening to his thought process, I again started to wonder about the intersection of creativity and logic. I decided my next goal was to answer the question I had stuck in my head: What is creativity's relationship with logic?

From your perspective, would you fill the following blank with "creativity" or with "logic?"

_____ *involves adaptability and how you react to given circumstances.*

I think both words work, but your own answer will vary depending on with what you attach yourself most.

Social conditioning has made us believe that these two facets are separate and distinct. However, creativity and logic work in coordination to achieve each other. Creativity is often thought to be synonymous with innovative thinking—but you can't achieve innovation without logic. These aspects are not opposites or independent of each other. Perhaps it is more of a spectrum; everyone has creativity and logic, but in different shapes and volumes.

A VISUAL ARTIST CREATING THROUGH EMOTION VS.
A COMPUTER SCIENTIST CREATING THROUGH LOGIC

Alex Baker was an enigma to me because of the way he could creatively problem-solve his emotional problems through logic. I do two things when I'm confused with a behavioral contingency: I bring Solomon with me and endlessly research on psychology websites.

Let's take a look at how Michael Levine explores the different facets of behavior and identity. Michael Levine is the founder of Levine Communications Office, one of America's "most prominent entertainment PR firms for the past thirty years." In terms of personal experience, he has represented, "more than seventy Academy Award and Grammy winners and over forty *New York Times* best-sellers."[25]

In his article on logic and emotion, Levine explores the different facets of human behavior and identity. He writes about "why people are who they are, do what they do, and what experiences, or lack thereof, are catalysts for their decision-making. All human brains have an emotional and logical side. People come in different proportions. Some are poets, and some are accountants, but we all have this in common—an unending strife in which both sides of our brains are locked in conflict at all times."[26]

Looking deeper into the article, he explains that the left side of the brain is more "pragmatic," and logical, while the right

---

25   Michael Levine, "Logic and Emotion," *Psychology Today*, July 12, 2012.
26   Ibid.

"puts up a dramatic fight for following the heart's content."[27] These characteristics, again, coincide with the escape room experience Alex and I had.

I think what amazes me most about Alex is not that I'm the complete opposite of him, but rather that statistically so many people don't work the same way he does. Levine explained that "emotions drive 80 percent of the choices Americans make, while practicality and objectivity only represent about 20 percent of decision-making."[28]

Consider this situation:

Bryant is finally buying his own place. He's worked hard on earning enough and finally decided to move out of his friend's garage. After days, weeks, and months of research, he finally finds a place in a great location. A place where the supermarket is just a two-minute walk away. The inside has a practical sized living room and enough bathrooms to support a future family. This house has everything that satisfies his practical *needs*.

The next morning, Bryant's real estate agent calls to inform him that there's another open house. After half an hour of looking, he realized that both of his choices are equally as good. In the area where one house was lacking, the other house made up for it.

Until he stepped into the backyard.

---

27 Ibid.

28 Ibid.

It was a blazing hot summer day, and the grass sat there bathing in the sun. There was a peach tree in one corner and a rusted bird bath on the other side. It reminded him of his mother's old house; of the times she would get so angry at the birds hanging out in the bird bath, even though that's what it was for.

To Bryant, this tree was the deciding factor. Until he saw the backyard, there were no stand-out characteristics for him to choose one house over the other. While both houses served equal practical needs, the second house provided subconscious comfort.

Months after he moved into the second house, he thought back to the day he signed his lease, when he was still hesitant about the decision. He laughed, now knowing there would be no length of commute or living room size that would trump the warm nostalgia of his mother's peach tree.

He knew that if he chose the first house, he would always be dreaming about the backyard that got away. In the end his decision was swayed more by the emotional tendencies of the right brain.

This would not be the same case for Alex.

He explained, "I'm a very logical thinker, so if there's a problem in my life, even if it's emotional, I think about it analytically instead of emotionally. I'll think, okay, this is the problem, these are things that I can do to solve it. If I follow through with this solution, this is likely to happen. If I pursue another solution, the other outcome is likely to happen. So I look at it in a cause-and-effect way. I ask myself, what can

I do now that will end up giving me the best benefit for the future? And coding is similar. Based on the parameters of the problem, you create an if-then statement. If one thing is true, then this will happen, and then you can follow the sequence of events. Following the cause-and-effect sequence to its end is what coding is, and is also the way I think."

I admired the way he was able to use the same coding cause-and-effect schema in working through his emotional problems. A mini-brain map of what this schema looks like can be generalized in a four-step framework:

1. Understanding the problem thoroughly and setting base parameters.

2. Listing actions that can be taken to potentially solve the problem.

3. Testing or imagining these different pathways.

4. Using the preferred pathway OR coming up with a new path through new knowledge learned from the failed imagined/tested pathway.

The main difference in the type of thinking is what each brain prioritizes. A right-brainer prioritizes relationships and moods and caters their solutions based on emotion. A left-brainer prioritizes logic and reason, getting each step done at a more efficient rate.

There are obviously individuals who are balanced in both facets of logic and emotion, although—as showcased in this chapter—people tend to lean toward one side more than the other.

After escaping the room, I was almost angry at myself that I hadn't learned this way of logical thinking earlier. After further research, though, I now believe that my emotions are indeed a key asset to my creative endeavors. I feel as though my driving force to create is how I *feel*. I work by embodying my emotions with prose or drawing, in hopes that my viewers might be able to relate and allow themselves to feel those feelings unapologetically, too.

Without tapping into my empathy and emotions, I wouldn't have created any of my pieces the same way. I can only wonder, with slight differences in my own schema, if those creations would have ever existed.

There's not a way to compare a logical thinker with an emotional thinker and say that one is better. Both serve a crucial role in human thought and help different processing and analyzing scenarios.

Creativity *needs* both logic and emotion.

Today I realize that the idea of processing emotions and feeling them is an essential part of my problem-solving and creative process. I could be logically thinking about the solutions and steps to unraveling my problems, but if I don't feel (keyword: *feel*) content with my decision, I let my feelings override my logical process.

For some, it may feel redundant or ridiculous, but there is power in executing decisions through feeling—to a reasonable extent, of course.

Because of the individual I am, I generally stick to solving all problems with emotional intelligence. I've found that what works for me is not to attack the problem directly or come up with my solution strategy right away, but rather to—first and foremost—cater toward my feelings. While it may seem "illogical," I've learned that it is critical for me to leverage my mood before confronting the issue.

An interaction between a right-dominant and left-dominant brainer might be extremely argumentative. Although the overarching goal is the same—regardless of which perspective it is analyzed through—the different steps taken might not necessarily be logically understood by an emotional being, and may not be emotionally understood by a logical person.

Again, this is not to segregate the left and right brain, because all the activities we do still utilizes both hemispheres—no matter how analytical or emotional an action may be.

EMPATHY'S RELATIONSHIP WITH CREATIVITY: APPARENTLY, THEY'RE MARRIED

Empathy is integral to creativity, according to an article from the National Center of Biotechnology Information (NCBI) regarding "The Differentiated Influence of Empathy on Different Magnitudes of Creativity."[29]

---

29 Sven Form and Christian Kaernbach, "More Is Not Always Better: The Differentiated Influence of Empathy on Different Magnitudes of Creativity," *Europe's Journal of Psychology*, vol. 14, 1 (March 2018): 54-65.

In the NCBI study, Sven Form and Christian Kaernbach explain that "empathy connects the creative person to the individual worlds of others."[30] Empathy helps individuals to be more aware in social contexts, allowing them to understand how other people feel. As a result, this increases a person's capacity to be creative because it adds another layer to consider when developing ideas.

To explain it in a different way, empathy allows the transfer of knowledge between people to happen more smoothly; and as mentioned in Chapter 1, that knowledge as well as imagination are two uniquely important components of creativity.

One example that shows how empathy plays a strong role in creativity is when "improving the quality of [a] creative product." This development process can then lead to understanding "the appreciation of the public perception of a product."[31]

Improving product quality is essential for innovators because their success relies on user satisfaction. For example, when creating an iPhone application, the user interface design is critical. App developers need to think about how to design their software around the preferences and aesthetics of their target market.

Minute differences in detail—such as rounded buttons versus harsh geometric shapes, or using sanguine versus crimson (similar yet distinct shades of red) in the color palette—have a huge impact on audience favorability. While these variations

---

30   Ibid.

31   Ibid.

may be undetectable to the regular user, they have proven subconscious effects.

In an article by Dalsukh Tapaniya titled "Colors in UI Design—Theory, Psychology & Practice," we learn more about the importance of color choice in design and its relationship to empathy and human psychology.[32]

The opening statement of Tapaniya's article illustrates that, as humans, we are constantly surrounded by colors. Every item we see exudes a color, and elicits a certain emotion; colors have the power to affect us in both mental and physical ways. To convey his thought, he points out that "to raise blood pressure, a strong red color has been shown, while a blue color has a calming effect."[33]

Tapaniya explains that "color is the easiest and most important aspect of engaging the user with the product in Design," but a lot of individuals believe that the colors chosen for the user interface is dependent on the subjective taste of the respective designer.[34]

However, color selection is a complex process in terms of the user interface. To elaborate on this topic, Tapaniya explains the psychology of color and includes a study by Joe Hallock, who works at Microsoft as a Principal Design Manager.[35]

---

32 Dalsukh Tapaniya, "Colors in UI Design—Theory, Psychology & Practice," *Medium*, May 26, 2019.

33 Ibid.

34 Ibid.

35 Ibid.

Joe Hallock's study, which demonstrates that "there is a significant difference in the choice of color between genders," collected data to see which colors were the most or least favorable. In his study, he finds that blue is "significantly favored by both men and women, and brown is the least liked color."[36]

The psychology of color helps designers gauge what speaks to different market segments: gender, race, and geographic locations. With evidence from these studies, when creating an application you can guess that more users will be inclined to like the blue-based user interface, compared to the brown one.

In order to design an effective interface, it is important to look closely at these minute characteristics—all of which require empathetic analysis and study.

Another illustration of empathy's relation to creativity is how it allows people to "identify strongly with fictitious characters in books, films, or plays."[37] Empathy opens up more opportunities for individuals to be inspired and create through their new understanding of a character. In a way, this idea of relating to fictitious characters is like being open to social connection. Even though these characters aren't real, they are still worth noting and relating to because they have lessons to learn from; they are built on the knowledge of the artist who created them.

My empathy allows me to dig deeper to understand why people feel and act the way they do. In turn, my understanding helps

---

36 Ibid.

37 Sven Form and Christian Kaernbach, "More Is Not Always Better: The Differentiated Influence of Empathy on Different Magnitudes of Creativity," *Europe's Journal of Psychology*, vol. 14, 1 (March 2018): 54-65.

me connect with others, to facilitate an honest conversation, learn about them, and learn from them. These three outcomes of empathy are essential for creativity, to build knowledge as a foundational basis, and to understand what to create for others.

When I fuse my interview with Alex with the research I've completed, we're left with the following takeaways:

1. The left hemisphere of the brain works in terms of logic, analytical thinking, and language.

2. The right works in emotion, creativity, and random thinking.

3. Both hemispheres work in coordination in order to function fully. No matter if someone is left- or right-brain dominant, we all always use both regions. This means that *everyone* is innately creative.

4. But there also has been some research saying that there is no brain dominance, and the brains of a mathematician and artist look the same in a brain scan. This theory *also* proves that everyone is innately creative.

5. Emotion and logic are two critical facets of creativity and decision-making. We require both, and there is beauty in both sides.

6. Emotion leads to creativity. Creativity leads to innovation. Innovations are the building blocks to our society. Therefore, the product of emotion can be felt and seen all around us, every day.

3

MY (NON-LINEAR, SQUIGGLY) CREATIVE PROCESS

Little Brothers & Play Pretends

The room we occupy would be dim,
lit by cloudy day spilling through a small window.
He'd pull up his computer and allow supernatural
theories to engulf him.

When sun finally sank into soil, the only
illumination in
the room would be his olive face, from the
reflection of the computer screen.
Between shadows seeping into creases of his
forehead and cheekbones,
He'd look exactly like our dad at seven.
He'd be an Angel.

Even with my absent-minded personality,
he'd force me to sit by the garden all day,
because apparently I needed to learn to open up,
and blooming flowers will teach me how.

In our rusty family photo albums, filled with
pictures and sticky surfaces,
there would be a picture of him chasing a goose,
with the same prominent cheekbones and wide
grey eyes.
He'd love plucking feathers from pillows
and birds.
He'd make me scrawny feather crowns from
peacocks and doves,
He'd use UHU super glue to stick them on his
back, right over the scapula, and say
"Look! I'm an Angel!"
(because he didn't already know his head was so
full of love
it glowed brighter than any halo).

Or maybe we'd fight all the time,
He'd rat on me if I snuck out past curfew.
Maybe he'd be a little devil,
and we wouldn't get along.
I wouldn't know.

I could continue and talk about his style,
but I'll keep that ambiguous—to build different
imaginations
for my only childhood self-indulgence.
I have no siblings, wish I did.

So I guess this leaves me filling blank
memories myself,
one feather at a time.

—Sam Budiartho

LEARNING HOW TO LEARN IN A LEFT-BRAINED WORLD

Growing up as an only child was why I started branching outward to facilitate my learning. In the absence of siblings, I was forced to be more inclined to seek others. Because of this, the friendships I form hold a special place in this gap—even though I wouldn't know what having a sibling is like, so I don't even know what hole I'm trying to fill.

These friendships and looking outward inevitably fueled (and still fuels) my creative process. Although sometimes I wish I had a sibling, I don't know how much that would impact me, or how many facets of my life would change.

On the bright side, my a) visual curiosity and b) empathy are two essential parts of my creative process, and, among other factors, they were both built through growing up as an only child.

A) VISUAL CURIOSITY

Throughout first through fourth grade, I was put into a developmental learning program. The program was built for students who fell behind in school; I struggled on many of the concepts that I was supposed to understand.

The majority of the students in my class found learning mathematics easy through rules, systems, and sequences. They learned math through first understanding the concepts, then applying them in multiple ways, many times over, to get faster and more comfortable with the process.

But that didn't really work for me.

I thought I was slow because I couldn't figure out how to excel like my other classmates could in this domain. But I wasn't bad at math; I was just taught these concepts in ways I couldn't readily understand. It took a very long and strenuous process to realize that my type of learning is different than those who were more math-inclined.

My mom, who always excelled in math, would be distraught because I couldn't figure out long division. I couldn't comprehend what it all meant or how it worked. It just didn't click for me; I couldn't understand how to solve 983 divided by 5 through a sequence or order.

In fact, both my parents are left-brain dominant thinkers. My dad majored in electrical engineering while my mom became an investment banker. It was hard to ask them for help on math homework because they were explaining it in ways that didn't fit well into my thought process.

My parents would explain that *983 was the dividend, and 5 was the divisor, and the problem itself was a quotient. When dividing the dividend with the divisor, sometimes the divisor doesn't divide evenly into the dividend and forms a remainder. There are four steps in long divis—*

That's where I would have to stop them.

I had to seek help from someone else, someone with a different perspective. In this situation, having a sibling would have theoretically increased the chances of being able to consult with another person in my direct family. But this doesn't necessarily mean that all siblings are helpful, or that every sibling dynamic is beneficial—I'm just saying that there is an *increased* chance for diverse support.

My only real solution was to find someone who thought in ways that were similar to mine. My family traveled a lot with our friends when I was younger, and that's when I became close to Kimberly. She's my parents' friends' daughter who used to babysit and feed me unlimited carrot cake.

When Kimberly realized I was struggling in school, she told me that we live in an analytical world. A lot of the time in schools, visual learners or right-brain dominant individuals are forced to change their natural thought process in order to adapt to the standardized way of teaching—through sequences, rules, and steps, an arduous task. She told me about an illustration of an elephant, bird, giraffe, and monkey gathered together in front of a tree. Facing them was a teacher who had a speech bubble saying, "To ensure a fair evaluation, everyone must take the same exam: Please climb that tree."

Who do you think would have the advantage here? This demonstrates the difference between *equality* and *equity*—for it to be a truly fair evaluation, the animals don't need equal chances at the same exam, but equitable tests.

Sometimes, I am an elephant in a world full of monkeys. I wouldn't be able to climb that tree no matter how hard I tried. However, once I realized I didn't have to follow my parents' way of thinking, I started understanding in ways I never thought I could.

I realized that as a visual learner, the fastest way I learn and understand information is through association. Initially, when learning a new concept, I don't have to force myself to use my left-brain to understand a math problem—even if the learning piece is a left-brain concept. Instead, I can use my right-brain and think of images and stories to understand a math problem.

This way, I finally could imagine the process of 983 divided by 5.

Nine Hundred, Eighty, and Three are all friends who live next to one another. Nine Hundred lives in the left section house, Eighty lives in the middle house, and Three lives on the right. Then one day, Five comes to visit each household, starting from left to the right. When Five comes over to Nine Hundred, another visual play comes around.

This way, visualization *shows* me how many times Five could fit into Nine Hundred, and then so on to the other neighbors. In the end, I have to combine all the numbers from each of the neighbors.

Easy!

Albeit complicated and long-winded when trying to do this for every long division problem. If I did, I probably would have imagined up to enough houses to solve the San Francisco housing crisis two times over. Thankfully, I didn't have to. Once I made this narrative, I was able to fully grasp long division. After understanding the concept visually through my right-brain, I was able to practice the act of doing long division "normally" with my left brain.

That same year, my teachers took me out of the developmental learning program.

I got good at functioning within the preliminary school system because I finally learned how to understand and take tests in my own way. It wasn't through order or sequence, but rather through pure visuals. Throughout high school, I would rewrite all my notes by hand and have them color-coordinated, with related doodles and drawings in different sections. While taking a test, I could just visually scan through the information in my notes, thinking about the colors as a cue for memory recall.

To be clear, no, I don't have photographic memory. Rather, my recall is enhanced when associated with color or imagery. After finding this special feature of my learning process, I realized that visuals would aid me to grow and lock in my understanding of concepts.

While I might be right-brained, it is important to remember that I still use concepts of the left brain. I grew up imitating a lot of traditional art—I acted, I drew, and I wrote a lot of poetry. All of which are right brain domains, right? Well, artists are good with proportions because they have an eye for the golden ratio—a mathematical concept. Poets write well because they have a good sense of technical linguistics—a left brain domain.

B) FEELINGS & EMPATHY

Being an only child, I slowly forced myself to be an extrovert at a young age to ease lingering feelings of loneliness. Because of this, I grew up being exposed to diverse personalities. From that, I grew up to be a very empathetic person. Today, it is easy for me to understand and respect why someone might feel or how they see things, even if I don't necessarily agree with their position.

Little did I know then this would be one of my most significant assets as a creator now. I feel as though when I create, I either try to convey an emotion that I have experienced and to in turn evoke that specific feeling from my viewers. All of a sudden, it becomes a game of trying to understand what visual stimuli evoke which emotions and piecing it all together through my own aesthetic to create art. Emotionally stimulating art.

Although I write a lot, I'm better at poetry compared to technical writing. For example, I wouldn't do as great a job trying to explain the function of a pencil compared to describing how love feels. Unfortunately and fortunately, I've grown up to be a sensitive and perceptive individual.

I am wired to be emotionally intelligent. I keep a database of feelings and spend a lot of time thinking and analyzing patterns of my own emotions and others. I think that emotions are a driving force of nature. A lot of what we do, think, and create is based on feeling. This is probably one of the biggest reasons why I'm a psychology major.

Being able to attach feelings to information allows me to understand theories further, and enables me to create and express art deeper than just surface level. In my letter to Mrs. Akira, I told her that I wanted the viewers of my artwork to *feel* something from it. How could I deliberately evoke those feelings without empathy?

Down to the smallest detail, my creative process has always been centered around emotion and feeling.

For example, writing this book has made me realize that while creating, I get lost in thought and emotions. Writing while I'm experiencing sadness, awe, or anger creates distinct tones on the page. I realize that it is difficult to emulate a certain vibe when feeling something else entirely.

Since I know I am receptive to emotions, especially when creating, I like to meticulously curate my playlist. Sometimes, I even listen to the same song on repeat until I'm done with a section. Why? Because it keeps the tone, mood, and flow constant throughout the written body. It's like I've created this little bubble of an environment to write effectively in that specific mood.

My journey of learning, and relearning, has taught me that there is no linear path. Continue doing your superstitious routine if you have one; start trying out different processes even if it may seem illogical to you. What sparks the flow of ideas is specific from one person to the next.

SEEING DIFFERENTLY WITH SYNESTHESIA

In this section, I want to express the importance of being comfortable in your own strange ways of thinking. This type of thinking is usually unconventional and sometimes not suitable for most people.

What better way to elaborate on unconventional thinking than writing a devoted section on synesthesia?

According to the frequently asked questions page of a Boston University project titled, "The Synesthesia Project," written by Dr. Veronica Gross, synesthesia "is loosely defined as *senses coming together.*" Most basically and at the "simplest level, synesthesia means that when a certain sense or part of a sense is activated, another unrelated sense or part of a sense is activated concurrently."[38]

For example, when someone sees a word, they see a specific color or shape that is always attributed to that specific word. Another example could be tasting a certain flavor and seeing a certain shape.

Some musicians, such as Pharrell Williams, have chromesthesia, the condition where music is associated with colors.[39]

---

38   Veronica Gross, "Frequently Asked Questions about Synesthesia," *Boston University,* accessed May 5, 2020.

39   NPR Staff, "Pharrell Williams on Juxtaposition and Seeing Sounds," *NPR,* December 31, 2013.

For individuals who have synesthesia, it can be quite a jarring experience when they start to realize that not everyone sees a color when hearing sounds or reading words.

I know from first-hand experience.

When I was younger, I wondered why "I" is yellow but an additional line creates "L" which is orange—after further research, I discovered grapheme-color-synesthesia. This condition causes individuals to involuntarily view words with specific colors consistently. But, of course, it varies between synesthetes.

My friend, let's call him Richard (we were way too young for me to remember his last name), and I debated for an hour if "bread" is emerald (it's *definitely* red). Personally, I see a light cast of color for each word, and similar colors are associated with analogous architecture such as hone and home, condemn and condom.

Growing up, reading and writing was not always easy for me—because of all the colors. Writing this piece or reading a book can be hard, especially when done aloud, because of all the colors distracting me. The word "red" is not actually red but a sky blue, which I always find extremely confusing to read. Another fun fact, the word "Satan" isn't a dark blood red or black—like you might imagine— it's actually hot pink.

For a long time, my Google Chrome history was filled with keywords like *color, synesthesia, weird, seeing, disease, disability, grapheme, involuntary, text, distraction.* I wasn't okay with this, so I hid my synesthesia for a long time, but I secretly used it in my art. I'd draw or write things with words that have similar colors, or even a pattern of colors.

I could've written a part of this section in a specific arrangement of colors, and you would never know. Beautiful. Chipmunk. Towel. Papercut. Scream. Sleep.

Around age seventeen, when I began to be more comfortable in embracing my synesthesia, it unfortunately started fading away. I finally received the ability to read quicker without distraction, in exchange for the gradual loss of my grapheme-color-synesthesia.

So I'm here to tell the uncomfortable syntesthetes, or the other thinkers and visualizers that believe their process is whacky and strange in a negative way—embrace it. Truly be proud of what you have because that's the way your brain functions and works the best, it is unique and the start of innovative thinking.

I cried a lot when I started losing my synesthesia. Always remember that what's taken for granted could eventually be taken away.

One topic always comes to my mind when talking about synesthesia and thinking differently: Patient S. What happens when an unlimited memory turns to reality? Meet nineteenth century patient "S.," also known as Solomon Shereshevsky. This particular case has been examined a multitude of times, heavily shaping the world of neuroscience throughout the nineteenth and twentieth centuries.[40]

---

40 Reed Johnson, "The Mystery of S., The Man with an Impossible Memory," *The New Yorker*, August 12, 2017.

With a photographic memory and thus the unlimited amount of information he could recall, S. rerouted scientific understandings of memory. His hardwired abnormalities made neurologists question all their previous assumptions. To put it simply, S.'s ability to remember everything was due to his intense synesthesia.[41]

S. was a Russian mnemonist who had a neurological "disease"—the inability to forget. Alexander Luria, a Soviet neuropsychologist, wrote a case study titled "The Mind of a Mnemonist," about S., after examining him for over thirty years.[42]

A *New Yorker* article entitled "The Mystery of S., The Man with an Impossible Memory," written by Reed Johnson, explains the first time S. found out about his unique synesthesia.

At the time, S. was a reporter for the Moscow Newspaper. One morning, during the editor's meeting with their reporters, the editor realized that S. just stood there, not taking a single note for his daily assignments. Later, when the editor came to scold S., S., "explained that he didn't need to write anything down." He simply remembered. The editor picked up a newspaper and read at length from it, challenging S. to repeat everything back to him. When S. did so—verbatim—the editor sent him to have his head examined."[43]

That's when Alexander Luria got involved. He began testing S.'s brain using concepts of synesthesia and memory palace

---

41 Ibid.
42 Ibid.
43 Ibid.

(a memorization strategy using visuals of familiar spaces to aid recall).

Luria wrote in the case study that S. had a strong type of synesthesia that crossed over more than two senses. In fact, it was the intensity of the associations that allowed S. to have unlimited recall of memorizing substances fast and for (what seemed like) forever.[44]

For example, to showcase his strong synesthesia, when Luria brought in a bell and rang it in front of S., he explained that the sound evoked "a small round object . . . something rough like a rope . . . the taste of salt water . . . and something white."[45]

Similarly, in S.'s unpublished notebook, a quote explained that "all the numbers had names, first and last, and nicknames, which changed depending on [his] age and mood." He then continued to explain that the numeral one "is a slender man with ramrod posture and a long face; 'two' is a plump lady with a complicated hairdo atop her head, clad in a velvet or silk dress with a train that trails behind her."[46]

Because of these mental images he was able to memorize random mathematical algorithms, excerpts from unfamiliar foreign languages, and random speeches for thirty years without recitation.

---

44   Ibid.

45   Ibid.

46   Ibid.

Besides his synesthesia, the mnemonist used something similar to a memory palace, by distributing images throughout an imagined physical space. His technique of walking through a neighborhood he was familiar with explains his ability to memorize a large amount of substance in order.[47]

Luria quickly realized that there was no maximum capacity of memory S. could hold, so instead he tried to search for drawbacks.

S. was unable to think in abstract ways the way a regular person would be able to. This, in turn, inhibited him from understanding the underlying meaning of metaphors or even recognize people's faces. S. complained that, "People's faces are constantly changing; it's the different shades of expression that confuse me and make it so hard to remember faces."[48]

Although this is an extreme case of synesthesia, it is worth noting that S. was able to execute these "super human" functions because he stuck to his mnemonic devices and embraced his synesthesia.

While we may not be able to have unlimited recall from thinking differently or unfolding our unique thought processes, we can nevertheless still learn about new ways of seeing.

These varied perspectives and methods will in turn enhance your innovative thinking.

---

47   Ibid.

48   A. R. Luria, *The Mind of a Mnemonist* (Cambridge: Harvard University Press, 1987), 64-66.

CREATIVE PROCESS: A KOI FISH FOR
THE ETHICS PROFESSOR

While writing this chapter, I couldn't decide if I wanted to showcase my creative process in terms of visual arts. Mainly because the book is meant to illustrate that the signifier "creative" extends beyond traditional art and artists. But then I realized that, as a visual artist, I know enough to explain that the process of developing art involves creativity even outside the physical act of drawing.

While I was analyzing my creative process, I had to tear apart the components of the process itself to fully understand its inner workings. I slowly started to see that when traditional artists explain their process, it is usually how they used a paintbrush to create a particular visual. However, that is only a slice of art creation.

The process starts with how you found the first source of inspiration, then continues all the way through spraying the piece with fixative or varnish. It's not only how your hands move when developing the artwork, but also what went through your brain to reach those artistic decisions.

It's how you pivot when you encounter a roadblock.

For example, in the summer of 2015, I had the opportunity to draw on people in New York (this was after Solomon and I had the Tuxedo Man as a visitor).

I explored most of my artistic talents that summer at Columbia University. I was there for the advanced creative writing program, but I think that was just a disguise. Life really put me there so I could explore my drawing practice. I doodled all over my legs with a pen every day, without fail. After day five, however, I realized that all my drawings looked the same. I was repeating the same animals and patterns. It had dawned on me then that it would be an interesting change to draw on strangers, but I didn't know how to start that conversation. I had to pivot, somehow; I had a problem, and now I had to find a solution.

To start exposing my art to others, I drew on friends who were also enrolled in the program. I started drawing on them in the courtyard, where a lot of people pass by. After a couple of days of quiet doodling, my makeshift tattoo parlor had gained some traction—students started coming to *me* asking for their own ink body art.

But even with the number of people I was drawing on, never did I think an Ethics and Religion professor would ask too.

At that point, it had become a mini-project, an improvised insight into the tattoo world. Now that I had succeeded in my quest to draw on strangers, I realized I needed to stop drawing the same patterns. So, I decided to play a free-association game with each of my subjects, trying to understand their thinking better even though they were strangers.

One by one they took a seat on Solomon and gave me a glimpse into their mind space. I wanted to draw something that somehow reflected a piece of themselves, but didn't want to take up too much time. We were all busy people, passing by one another between lectures and workshops.

During the free-association exercise, I'd say one word, and they would reply with another. This exchange of words would go on for a couple minutes, and, after, I would sit and think about which words I would use to develop a visual.

With the Ethics and Religion professor, I distinctly remember this subsection of the word exchange:

I started with "innovation," he replied "light bulb."

I said "wildlife," he said "fish."

I said "clothing," he said "suit and tie."

I said "preposition," he said "inside"—among other words in exchange, these four sets became the central premise of the image I was about to devise. In the end, on his forearm, I drew a hanging light bulb with a koi fish wearing a suit and tie, swimming inside the glass.

The creative process is more than just the drawing itself. It is the intersection of the very first seed, the very last person receiving a pen tattoo, and everything that happened in between. This is often overlooked.

Without empathy and emotional intelligence, I would have never been able to successfully connect in that setting with that many people on a level beyond mere small talk.

By the end of the summer program, a total of forty-eight people sat on Solomon as I drew on their skin. Before I drew on anyone, I first had to be in an active conversation with them. From these few moments forward, I started practicing different forms of illustration and honing my creative process.

COLLABORATION: TO BUILD A HOME WITH LIPSTICK

When doing a collaboration, it is so refreshing to see the solutions that arise when two brains work together. Two different, varied, and passionate brains fuse together to find the best solution. It is a perfect environment for the meaningful transfer of knowledge to happen.

One collaboration that changed the way I viewed art was a spontaneous personal art project called, *To Build A Home* (Figures 2 & 3). It all started when I met Nisha Khater. Nisha lived in Bangladesh before she moved to Indonesia in her junior year of high school. We became friends during that time and instantly clicked as artists. Not long after we met, Nisha and I decided that the art project would entail drawing on someone's back. To this day, I am still thankful that the model in the images below, Charl Fourie, said yes. In this context of collaboration, Nisha was the photographer, while I was in charge of drawing on Charl.

Nisha believes that her right brain is more dominant in the way she thinks, acts, and creates. In her own words she explains, "I think that I'm a little less analytical in a sense. In terms of thinking and expressing, I believe that my right brain is activated more. I love the sciences and math, but I think the way I behave and perceive the world is a lot more visual than analytical."

Again, it is important not to be fooled about hemisphere dominance. Even though she is a phenomenal photographer and leans toward the right brain, she is also currently studying computer science at Brown University.

Regarding her major, Nisha says, "The reason that I chose computer science is because there are many ways of approaching problems. There is no specific right path to the solution. I love that you can be creative and solve problems in your own way, and still apply that to the analytical thinking side."

Just like Alex Baker, the computer science major from the previous chapter, Nisha believes that her field involves a lot of creativity.

When I asked Nisha to look back on the *To Build A Home* collaboration, she said, "Moving was a little bit difficult for me. Especially moving from a place that was home to me made it difficult to adjust. I think that's where the concept of *To Build A Home* really came in."

Nisha and I were merely two artists who wanted to collaborate. Throughout the process, it was a constant give and take. There were some ideas we both loved, some we disagreed with, and some we'd never even think of without the other.

When collaborating, you take two brains that have experienced entirely different lives and give them a new, empty host to live in. That host then grows into collaborative art.

When we first started talking, Nisha and I bonded over moving around different countries and naturally the song *To Build A Home* by Cinematic Orchestra came up.

The song and the idea of "home" became the anchor of our inspiration. In relation to this concept of home, Nisha explained that, "It takes a lot more than a physical location and a physical standing structure to call somewhere your home. Instead it's something you have to create for yourself. You have to be vulnerable and really open to making that lifestyle and experience for yourself and making that place a home for you."

We decided that the photos would be taken at a (possibly haunted) abandoned house. Nisha elaborated on the chosen location by saying that "the abandoned house was perfect because it wasn't this beautifully decorated home, but something really raw and just symbolized the idea that home is not the structure but rather the feeling. Feeling comfortable, vulnerable, and happy within that space."

After we decided on the location, Nisha and I needed a subject to draw. What would symbolize the idea of the self so we could place those images inside the abandoned house?

During that time, I was really big on anatomical hearts—I had just had to memorize the different parts of it for my biology class. Through this sectioned piece of paper (Figure 1), I was able to visualize the different parts when I took my test (again, as a visual learner, it may seem like a lot of work, but it goes a long way). The visual realm holds an essential place in my recall, attention, and understanding.

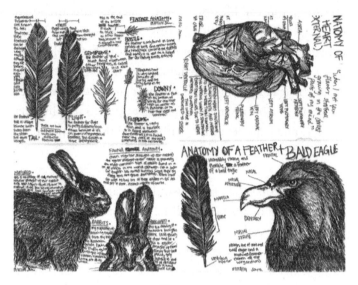

Figure 1.

Thus, the anatomical heart idea just fell into our laps. We decided that the heart would fit well with the idea of the self.

The next part of our process was a more difficult one. How could we draw on someone's back without giving them a nasty allergic reaction to harsh chemicals like acrylic paint? We gravitated toward makeup as our solution.

Before I start any of my creative processes, I take time to think it through visually in my head. At this point, I had already decided on the tools I wanted to use, and then thought about which tool could create which effect:

- Crayon eyeliner = to create smooth outline edges.

- Mascara applicator = to develop texture and shading from the dark outlines to the lighter insides.

- Liquid eyeliner = to generate form, veins, and harsher lines.

- Red lipstick = to outline the veins of the heart for both color and dimension.

Since this piece was drawn on a human back, when the person moved, the heart drawing bent, distorting its shape and producing a unique moment that could never be replicated.

In this piece, my creativity was not only expressed through drawing, the same way Nisha's creativity was not only conveyed in taking the photographs. It was also used in figuring out how to draw the heart on a surface that wasn't flat, on skin. It was used when I had to be efficient in my strokes because the model was continually sweating off the makeup. It was also used in locating and trying to get into the abandoned house. And also, in being able to photograph without studio lighting.

Here, creativity was represented by far more than just a drawing and the click of a button.

TO BUILD A HOME, 2015

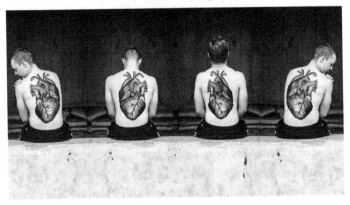

Figure 2.

Figure 3.

INTEGRATION OF DOMAINS: THE MAN WITH TWO FACES

Why do our brains function the way they do? How do our personalities differ depending on our moods? Strangely enough, it was these psychological questions that pushed me to develop portraits. I've always used drawings as a learning technique to develop a deeper understanding of the subject. While this may work for an anatomical heart or the skeleton of the human body, it doesn't really translate with something more profound, such as the personality we showcase to others versus when we're alone.

But alas, I went for it anyway.

Combining two different mediums of knowledge has always been the most exciting way to learn for me. This new project was a golden opportunity to learn more about both psychological theories and the technique of hyper-realism with charcoal. I started to curate and develop a series in hopes to understand the segregation between our inner and outer selves; the personalities we show and hide. I decided that the first image of the series (Figure 4) would simply be a hyper-realistic portrait, without distortions—a sort of "control" sample.

I decided that if I wanted to fully commit to this project, I had to learn how to create a hyper-realistic piece in my own style.

I had to adjust to the situation. A lot. Charcoal was a new medium to me, especially with a big canvas. I had to learn to work with tools like cotton buds and weirdly shaped erasers (so I could create precise blending tools). The hair in the portraits was simple to illustrate, but only once I found a solution for how to develop the illusion of hair stands without actually drawing every individual strand.

With trial and error, I found the fastest way. After blacking out the hair area with a charcoal stick, I had to cut a very sharp edge from my eraser then went back in with it to create the strands. I filled up the black area by erasing a variation of wavy and straight lines—all in all, it took about five minutes.

After completing the first portrait, I wanted to create another one with an added element of distortion. The distortion (seen in Figure 5) conveys the two sides to every person: the outer and the inner. The truth is hidden underneath a façade of the outward self when we are with others.

In today's advanced and evolving society, it's easy for individuals to create something eye-catching, but it's harder to make someone stop and think. As an artist, I want to illustrate different psychological phenomenon and question uncomfortable topics.

INT(RA)PERSONAL, 2017 (32 X 22 IN)

Figure 4.

INT(ER)PERSONAL, 2017 (32 x 22 IN)

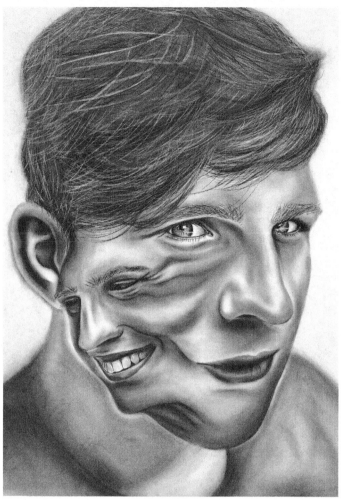

Figure 5.

I started moving away from hyperrealism art to surrealistic hyperrealism.

Once I was able to master precision in these drawings, I wanted to illustrate something that existed beyond the real world. I wanted to convert the crazy dreams and visuals in my imagination and turn them into something meaningful, for others to experience.

And thus, my tryptic *dear society* (Figures 6, 7 & 8) was born.

dear society stems from a painful, yet integral, part of my self-identity. Throughout my life, others' intentions of love were lost in translation and instead became the reason for my self-hate. This form of love was to mold me to better fit into society, where fame, riches, and looking like an "Asian Barbie Doll" are priorities.

Through this, though, I gained clarity in finding my self-worth in resisting these norms, and understanding that my true identity and beliefs are valid and vital. In the first panel (Figure 6), the large charcoal eye depicts strength. It visualizes that despite all the negative influences around me, I am still open-eyed and alert to my own self-worth.

The second panel (Figure 7) conveys the society's "surveillance" aspect. All the eyes look inward toward the actual, physical mirror. When viewers stand in front of the mirror, all the eyes are judging their reflection. These eyes are cry-out to voice the concept that the social constructs we've created to survive can simultaneously be ones we hate.

The final panel (Figure 8) is a rolled back eye. This eye represents all the individuals who were pushed to societal conformation; though they gain social acceptance, they are unhappy and empty inside. I recognize that I, myself, am a part of this society, which is represented through the conjoined eye folds from the first panel to the last. But I also often disagree with the societal beliefs—here communicated through the physical gaps between each panel.

The deep meaning, information, and backstory are simply illustrated through eight eyes. This is because I once awoke from a painfully vivid nightmare about a blob monster with endless eyes. I woke up thinking it would be an interesting visual, and asked myself what it could mean.

DEAR SOCIETY, 2019 (TRYPTIC 24 X 60 IN)

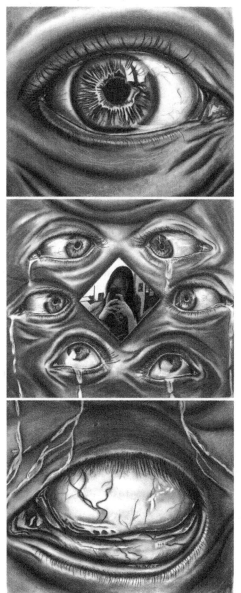

Figure 6, 7, 8.

Personally, it's more rewarding to create something that doesn't already exist. This way, the creation is built from what's stored in my imagination. Imagination, of course, comes from our subjective thoughts, but it also incorporates the influences of others. The way you hear and process information from one person would be different from another person.

There are no boundaries when creating art, so why confine yourself? Art is just understanding the various facets of this world and then making something from them. It can involve any medium: ink, blood, flowers, car parts. Building cars, building houses, building a website—these are all different forms of art, too. The more you believe in this concept, the more open-minded you'll be the next time you create.

When trying to verbally explain your vision or plan to someone, that person is usually visualizing it in a totally different way. Nothing is going to look the same between one imagination and another. You could be imagining a wolf with three eyes, but the images that could fit that criteria are endless and expansive.

It can be a wolf with toes as eyes, or it can be a wolf with those three eyes floating above its head—those pieces are never going to look the same from one mind to the next. That's the beautiful part of art; what you create is never going to be the same as someone else's. It's like two different people reading the same book; they're going to read the same words but play different visuals in their heads.

Being able to translate what is in your mind onto paper is an inexplicable, valuable tool. Using it, I wanted to be able to translate my dreams to paper to show what they looked like. This pathway was the main driving force for me to continue practicing hyperrealism.

Throughout analyzing my creative process, I learned that:

- It may be necessary to move away from how we were taught to learn, to find a way that is more efficient for us. It took me a while to realize that I learn best through visual curiosity and empathy.

- As a visual artist, creativity is used in ways that are more than just the physical act of creation:

  - It greatly involves how you adjust and re-gear when hitting a dead end.

  - It's the process of finding innovative solutions to inevitable problems.

- Collaborations go a long way in developing our creative assets. It allows us to think through another brain, which is the perfect environment for knowledge transferal.

- Integrating two disciplines into one project sparks innovation.

  - Be open and receptive to absurd thoughts and dreams,

    - They are a rush of inspiration in disguise.

4

ANALYZING (ENGINEERS' & PHOTOGRAPHERS') CREATIVITY

———

434

Dear Alice,
Every morning, he wakes up at four thirty-four,
drinks four shots of espresso with three-fourths
    of a sugar sachet,
runs four miles in thirty-four minutes.
Every afternoon, he tunes in to channel four three
    four, listening to electronic-blues.
Every night, he dials in +1 (434) 386-6108 to say
    his prayers to his mom in Virginia.
And every day he strives to be consistent with his
    routine
because it's the only thing he can control between
    the spontaneous world and the
unpredictability of our feelings.

"I fear that one day she'll wake up and throw it all away."

—Sam Budiartho

CREATIVITY IS NOT ALWAYS COMFORTABLE

Consistency. The majority of us prioritize consistency because we fear the unknown. Think about this scenario: you're home alone. You hear a soft and eerie scratching in the corner of the room. You start freaking out, not because of the sound itself, but because you don't know the *source* of the sound. Once you find out it's actually just the generator from the other room, the sound doesn't scare you anymore. You feel more at peace from knowing, more comfortable because the unfamiliar becomes less foreign.

As humans, we simply prefer the familiar over the unknown—but our fears and the unknown are important spaces to visit when unlearning "creativity." Since we have been predisposed to learn along a linear path, we become comfortable in our habits, we start thinking in a one-dimensional form. We are unable to think in new ways because the brain is consistently rewarded with comfort when staying within embedded habits. A risk-reward relationship is needed for learning, growing, and innovative thinking.

It is essential to confront our fears because they facilitate creative thinking; these foreign places help us find new knowledge and ways to imagine: the keys to creativity. The unknown is an undiluted, unlimited space to grow; it is the odyssey to find new understandings, answers, and perspectives. When we face our fears, we may not always find the realizations or perspectives for which we're searching. But that's the beauty of it. It's hard to anticipate and fathom what you might learn, until you go look for yourself.

No two creative processes are the same, because of the unique backbones of knowledge and imagination we all have. What one person might experience as an unknown, another could be extremely familiar with it. While the unknown ranges from one individual to another, what's important to note is not the topic itself, but rather what they do to confront that topic—and how they fuse it into their creative processes.

Let me share a little story of Jacan, the person who planted the idea of embracing our fears in my head. Ever since that day, I've been actively trying to confront my discomfort with the unknown, to push myself toward new knowledge, perspectives, and realizations.

FEAR AS A DRIVING FORCE

It was December 22, 2017, and I was at the peak of Calabasas, a 2,163-foot summit in California. I was breathless from both the view and the sweaty hike. As I stood on this elevated throne, I was able to see cloud shadow effortlessly roaming the valley, trees that intertwined, and mountain ridges that lazily bathed in the sun.

I thought the view was the golden treat of it all, but I was naïve.

As I approached the American flag posted at the absolute peak of the hike, I stumbled upon a red distressed notebook. Being intrigued and nosey, I flipped through the empty pages until I found a trace of ink and read:

"I don't really know what to say as I've been blown away by the beauty of nature today. So I guess I'll try to leave some wisdom. I used to think that the greatest human achievement was to have your name remembered and passed down in history, thus immortalizing your legacy. Now I feel that we must embrace our moral selves and enjoy the beauty that is physical life. Be content with silence, because in the end, we all die alone, but that is nothing to be afraid of. Fear is the mind-killer, so embrace it"

— JACAN, PEACE & LOVE, 12-20-2017.

Here's the original picture, to give Jacan his full justice:

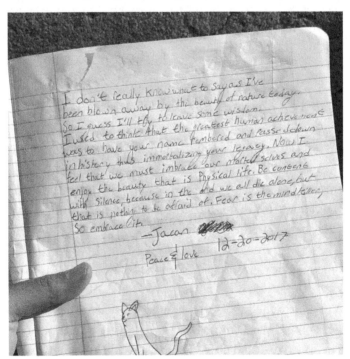

Figure 9.

I wish I knew Jacan, so I could fully give him credit for leaving behind something so important and honest. Without the last name or social media handle attached to the piece, I am unable to trace who this person is. Jacan genuinely meant what he wrote about living in the physical now and not worrying about immortalizing his name. He wrote his feelings down and left it for anyone who picked up the notebook. It was refreshing that the writer didn't want credit, even though Los Angeles is full of people who self-promote at any given chance.

It's crazy to think that Jacan was only there two days before I was. This is probably the fifth or millionth time I've said this, but life has its unexpected ways of delivering lessons.

I recognized that "Fear is the mind-killer" is a quote from author Frank Herbert, who wrote the novel *Dune*.[49] Fear constricts our creative endeavors because it hinders us from diving into the unknown, into discomfort. A lot of the time, we'd rather stay at home in our comfortable nooks and crannies, a narrative all too familiar for most humans.

In a perfect world, we would grow through serene and snug places, but we all know that growth usually comes from an invasive place. It comes from a place that confronts you with burdensome questions, a place that may break you and ask you to drag your mind and body through bitterness. But thankfully, sometimes if you let it hurt just a little, you'll work toward finding self-actualization and a deeper connection to creativity. Reflect on last year. Doesn't it feel like so much

---

49   Frank Herbert, *Dune* (London: New English Library, 1972.)

has changed? Haven't your creative and thinking processes changed significantly?

If they have, that's probably because somewhere along the way you said: fuck it, let's dive into open water, devoid of nearby islands.

The following section is primarily devoted to illustrating the innovative processes of traditional and non-traditional artists: two female engineers and two male photographers. I've conducted interviews in hopes to analyze their thinking processes and prove the point that engineers are just as creative as photographers, thus showcasing that the only difference between the two career paths is the medium—not the level of creativity.

CREATIVITY IN MECHANICAL ENGINEERING & PHOTOGRAPHY

NAJWA BOU-MELHEM: THE METICULOUS ENGINEER

As we grow in the world, we get to meet people throughout different parts of our lives; these different parts could pertain to periods, locations, or settings. But it's always a shock when two of your friends, from these different parts, somehow are tied together. The story of how I met Najwa is one such entwining.

In my senior year of high school, I knew of a girl who previously went to school in Saudi Arabia. There, she met Najwa Bou-Melhem. By that time, Najwa had left Saudi Arabia for Morocco, while our mutual friend and I were in Indonesia. When college acceptances started rolling in, Najwa and I both got accepted and committed to the University of Southern California. At this point, we saw each other's names on social media as #usc2022 incoming freshmen and vaguely recognized one another from our mutual friend's Instagram account. In the end, Najwa and I ended up being suitemates.

I couldn't be happier that we agreed to do so because today we've grown and sworn to be the best of friends. Sorry if you've grown bored of this phrase, but life has its strange ways of delivering important people.

The sun was scorching down on us when we first met. We stood in line, squished between other incoming freshmen bodies, waiting to receive student orientation packets. Although it was a new space filled with unfamiliar faces, I felt strange comfort from Najwa standing beside me (even though we'd only met a couple minutes earlier).

It wasn't long before she started calling me Samsonite, and let me sleep in her bed when I had sleep paralysis—and frankly, when I just wanted to.

To introduce Najwa a little bit, she's half-Lebanese and half-Moroccan, and is pursuing an engineering degree. I know for a fact that we would both characterize her as hard-working, passionate, lively, and self-critical. Before I asked to interview her, I'd actually been sending her my second drafts of each chapter of this book. Even though she's a busy woman and is not at all obligated to give me feedback, she still spent hours on editing calls with me. She helped me navigate abstract thoughts into concrete words because our thought processes are similar—despite the fact that I specialize in two-dimensional art and design, while she specializes in engineering.

When I started the interview, I first asked how she sees the world. It's a heavy subject disguised as a brain teaser, and the same opening question I ask all my interviewees.

She replied, "I constantly go back and forth between believing that humans have predestined paths and believing that every occurrence is random. I feel like I don't have enough proof to sway me one way or another. It's like I believe both and neither at the same time."

The reason I ask this question is to gauge how my interviewees experience the world—a component that heavily affects the inner working of their lives and which directly influences their creative processes. Since Najwa has no reason to believe in either a predestined or free-for-all life, she consistently allows herself to be receptive and open-minded to all possibilities.

She continued, "Historical documentaries seem like fiction to me because life was so completely different in the past. However, people like me actually existed in those forms once upon a time." Can you imagine how creative our past individuals had to be to redefine society and the way of living while facing their own disasters?

Moving on from our past collective creativity, I asked her if she thinks what she does is creative; is engineering a form of creative work?

She answered, "Engineering can essentially be defined as the science of creation, making it an inherently creative practice. I am a mechanical engineering major, so I use engineering principles to design and build machinery. A lot of my assignments are problem-based; therefore, I am instructed to create a solution for a given issue." Her version of problem solving is no different than the creative process of a traditional artist. Where engineering is the science of creation, the visual arts, for example, can be considered as the creation of a visually appreciated object.

To break down her creative process, she explained, "I take the physical laws that I've learned and combine them with design principles in order to solve the problem within the given constraints. However, just satisfying the requirements is not enough in such a competitive field; I must think outside the box to incorporate extra value into my solution." The first point to note is that, because of our evolving world, every discipline is no longer singular. They are all now interdisciplinary, to an extent.

For example, her engineering work involves the principles of design, while the development of my visual art involves mathematical models for angles and proportions. We both use both.

There are three components to her creative process, which can be generalized and outlined as:

- Being exposed to and learning about a specific field.

- Combining her knowledge and inventiveness to develop a solution.

- Thinking outside of the box to incorporate extra value.

I believe that all successful career paths involve all of these bullet-points, no matter which one. Another way to present the three factors is through the definition of creativity, which again, for the purposes of this book, is the integration of knowledge and imagination. While the first part of her creative process alludes to knowledge and the last to imagination, the middle step is the intersection between the two.

To exemplify innovative thinking, she explained, "This can be done by using a never-before-seen structure or technology, by integrating an additional function, or by producing something completely unpredictable. In an ever-advancing industry, you must be innovative to compete, which requires creative thinking every step of the way."

I've noticed that Najwa is a meticulous planner—whether that is when she works on her college assignments, or plans to go to the beach. Najwa will not move forward into the meat of an endeavor until she is completely done planning every crevice and corner. When you plan ahead, you work effectively, and have enough time to be inspired and think of innovative ideas.

When I asked Najwa about her thinking processes, she explained, "If there's one word no one would ever use to describe me it would probably be spontaneous. I usually spend more time planning than most, which I see as a worthy investment because the extra time I spend preparing takes away time I would have wasted while working without direction. This goes for whatever creative endeavor I pursue; when I write, my outlines are meticulous, when I build, my designs are thorough, and when I cook, my process is already precisely predefined. With that said, I believe some of the best ideas can come on impulse, so I'm careful not to restrict my freedom to explore different ideas that come to me while creating."

This planning frenzy of hers will not be everyone's cup of tea—it is *her* unique way of thinking and navigating her creativity. When we look at what work an individual does, it isn't about gauging the amount of creativity put into it, rather it's about understanding the different mediums in implementing creative thought.

To prove Najwa's mechanical engineering creativity, I'm going to compare and contrast the three components of her creative process with Tim Tan, a photographer and conceptual artist.

TIM TAN: THE ECCENTRIC PHOTOGRAPHER & CONCEPTUAL ARTIST
I first met Tim at an obscure coffee shop in Indonesia where he was visiting at the time. I wasn't expecting to see him there, but I'm happy that the universe let our paths meet. Thinking back, it was just two different types of creators sitting together, discussing how the different ways we create energizes us more than cups of coffee.

"I think, I think a lot about thinking a lot," was the line that caught me when I asked Tim how he sees the world.

Tim Tan is a twenty-eight-year-old Singaporean who has been stepping up in the photography industry; he is an artist who does not limit himself to thinking in one lateral dimension. He's famously known for his gif-moving photography and project titled PERSPECgifs, that alters the viewer's perception. He's shot artists like Charli XCX, Rich Brian, The Higher Brothers, and more; his works can be found on his Instagram handle, @perspecgifs and @imtimtan.

Tim has dropped out of art school, twice (and high school once). He believes that we lose our liberty toward greater understanding within rigid education systems. You're taught what to think, so you end up solving problems in only one way.

Regarding his learning process, Tim explains that his "is a bit strange, and it's not really well made for school, because I do it internally. When I was younger I did more alternative forms of learning. When people were going to kindergarten, I was going to Montessori. In Montessori, it's like a more kinesthetic form of learning that really encouraged being curious." He explained he was taught the same things as the traditional kindergarten setting, but in each individual's own way and pace.

Growing up, he'd have a LEGO set with a pamphlet of instructions, but he'd refuse to follow any of them and do it an entirely different way. That's how his art began. It began with him thinking "outside of the box," yet he doesn't really like this distinction—it implies that there was a box to begin with.

He started going out more to see artistic creations, yearning to learn the visual language. This can be likened to mechanical engineer Najwa's first step into her creative process, which is exposing herself to learn about a specific field. In his context, Tim started exploring him creative self via the visual arts.

Tim didn't want to be one of those curators who looked at an abstract piece and goes, "I don't get it." He wanted to learn the language; he felt like it was a secret code to crack. Years later, after he started learning about visual stimulation through art galleries, he began thinking about his personal visual language.

After years of schooling and conditioning, a lot of individuals follow rules on being creative; the equation of x, y, and z allows us to be creative. But, as you may have guessed by now, it is imperative to unlearn this definition of creativity. As a man who has ADHD and partial dyslexia, Tim believes unconventional approaches adds to his creative thinking.

Tim explained that he's always been the type of person that lacks visual stimulation. This is why he has always needed multiple things going on at once, to keep him interested. He said, "If you've ever seen my computer setup, I have three screens, and I'm doing work on all three of them. I've been known to play three computer games at the same time. It's just a different way of the stimulation of ideas."

He then began researching theories and how 3D films work. In our discussion about perception, he said that "when I was painting geometric abstract art, I was thinking to myself about how I could suggest something beyond the viewers. How I could suggest something to the viewer, based on perception. Force them to see and use perception to control the viewer."

For about five years, Tim had been playing with concepts of auto-suggestion for his art's audience and understanding how subliminal suggestion could impact a person's vision gravely. The way he created his phenomenal gif-images is through stereoscopy, also known as stereo imaging. This technique was developed in the non-digital form of film photography. It is the process that allows images to have an increased perception of depth, basically creating an illusionistic 3D result.[50]

In his practice Tim takes a couple of photographs of the same subject but tweaks the angles slightly. He shifts his film camera's perspective little by little, then sandwiches the files into one clip. Tim was obsessed with the idea of being able to suggest depth with basically nothing and discovered that through stereoscopy, the subject would pop out of the canvas just enough for the brain encode the image as three-dimensional.

This section of Tim's creative process parallels Najwa's second component, which is combining her knowledge and inventiveness to develop a solution. In his own context, Tim's "problem" was figuring out a way to play with perspective, and his "solution" was stereoscopy—but he would never have arrived at that conclusion without the combination of technical film knowledge and imagination to develop conceptually captivating photographs.

When I asked Tim how he gets inspired to create, he explained, "I don't really like the idea of inspiration from another artist. I think to be inspired by something means that you kind of have been influenced with someone else's idea. Often, I'll try

---

50 *Encyclopaedia Britannica Online,* Technology ed., s.v. "History of Photography," accessed May 5, 2020.

to not look at a lot of work for a long period of time so that I come up with what I feel is my pure creation, to an extent. I will try to be away from a lot of pieces of work so that I don't get accidentally subconsciously influenced. Instead, I like to tap into my curiosity. Often the seeds are just very subconsciously placed. It just kind of happens."

Even though he tries to stray away from others' work while he creates, he clarifies, "I think it's still very important to be open to ideas and see what people are doing. Yet when creating, I wish to be clear of all influences. It's a bit paradoxical."

It was eye-opening to hear Tim's analysis of his own creative thinking; I definitely found some overlap with mine. As mentioned in the previous chapter, I'm open and receptive to my absurd thoughts and dreams because to me they are a rush of inspiration in disguise.

The idea of Tim and I being receptive to our wacky thoughts, in turn, connects back to Najwa's final component of her creative process, which is thinking outside of the box to incorporate extra value. While all of us may utilize this component in our creative processes, it's important to realize that we all do it in our own specific ways—with what inherently works for our differently wired brains.

On the topic of inspiration, he continued, "I'm always thinking to myself, like, fuck, I definitely want to see something like this, or I want to embody this idea I have in my head. So I'm looking for the patterns that spark my brain, actively searching while trying to be open and aware of the sparks around me."

While Najwa and Tim are pursuing very different career paths, they both use an equal amount of creativity—they just exemplify two separate mediums. Although the generalized backbone of all our thinking processes may be the same, they are nevertheless all intensely unique and curated via our own inner workings.

To reiterate this conclusion, let's look at another set of individuals pursuing contrasting career paths.

CREATIVITY IN COMPUTER SCIENCE & PORTRAIT PHOTOGRAPHY

KIARA TANOJO: THE EMPATHIC COMPUTER SCIENTIST

I had just moved from Singapore to Indonesia to attend Jakarta Intercultural School. It was my first day there when I met Kiara Tanojo. We were ten years old. The memory is definitely faulty, but from what I can recall, it was during the rainy season; I had moved in halfway through the year, in January. I want to say that we met at "drop off," the area all the kids would sit at after school and wait for their parents or drivers to pick them up. I also want to say that I probably initiated the conversation because Kiara has always been more introverted.

But what I can confidently say is that Kiara was the first real friend I made in Jakarta. We made code names for the different boys we admired from a distance, took our first sips of alcohol, and walked down the auditorium for our high school graduation together. Although we currently attend colleges in different states, we know we can always rely on each other, no matter the distance.

Our friendship might be strange because we aren't very similar individuals in the way we think and process information—but again, that doesn't negate the creativity in either of us. I remember struggling with fifth grade math and always asking Kiara for help. Even though we think differently, Kiara's deeply rooted empathy allowed her to explain it in terms that I could understand.

To introduce Kiara, she's Indonesian and goes to the University of Michigan in pursuit of computer science. She explained, "I would say I like to challenge myself and be competitive, because I want to be the best that I can possibly be. If that makes sense...I hope that's not really cheesy. I also would always prefer tests over projects, and I would definitely take a math test over a humanities paper any day." She's one of those people who doesn't ever procrastinate, even if she says she does.

She's diligent, analytical, empathetic, and is a great teacher (thank you for your patience when I asked you such rudimentary AP Calculus questions).

When I asked her if she thinks computer science involves creativity, she replied, "The hardest part about computer science is being able to train your brain to think in different ways. There are always many ways to implement a solution, but sometimes our brains are geared to think there is only one solution. It's hard to solve a problem when you think narrow-mindedly asking 'what's the answer?' instead of taking a step back and asking 'how should I answer?'—and I think that's what makes it creative."

Kiara's definition of creativity overlaps with mine: the process of finding innovative solutions to problems by adapting yourself to think differently. While Kiara uses creativity to see in new perspectives and solve problems in computer science terms, I use new perspectives to develop interesting visual nuances in my art.

When I asked her to explain how she confronts problems, in hopes to further understand her creative process, she explained, "In the beginning I always thought 'how would you even approach this question?' But I've learned that sometimes you have to look at the problems and try finding the easiest way to solve it before using more complex layers of processing." Kiara actively takes apart these intricate and complicated problems to understand their sum parts at a simplified level. To efficiently think this way, she has to be receptive and adapt to new perspectives—meshing her past experiences with the context of the given problem.

She continued to explain her process in regard to taking complex material apart, "I break down the problem into smaller pieces, trying to understand the base case problem. After I understand the easiest problem, I then shift my perspective on how that simple situation can branch out into bigger, more complicated problems. It is always important to look at the roots."

Creative and divergent thinking involves breaking apart these large ideas to understand and analyze the smaller part and backbone of the problem. Using our previous knowledge and imagination, when looking at the smaller units, we are able to spawn unique solutions. This is exactly what Kiara implements throughout her process of solving a question in math and engineering.

Furthermore, this idea of breaking apart larger ideas is also heavily utilized within the realm of two-dimensional art and design. For example, when I first learned how to draw hyper-realistic portraits, I often got overwhelmed at all the nuances they contained. If you asked people to think about the middle stages between a blank starting page and a hyper-realistic artwork, chances are they wouldn't know where to start. But if you asked someone to take a step back and think about it in logical terms, every person, no matter the medium, knows that progress starts from breaking up the bigger picture into smaller components.

Developing these small parts comes with finding more efficient ways, or "solutions," to draw the different parts, and sometimes even to see the whole piece in a different light and completely change the aesthetics.

Kiara and I use different mediums to exude our creativity and flexible thinking.

She continued, "I definitely think that you do need to delve into things that are unknown to really create something that's new. With some specific algorithms, they solve the same problem but they're just executed in different ways. Those different ways don't just come naturally, you kind of have to step outside your comfort zone. That also is important in terms of creativity." Kiara reiterates the beginning of this chapter: that facing our fears and the unknown is an essential part of acquiring new knowledge to implement creativity.

Throughout the interview, Kiara highlighted the important parts of her creative process, which can be simplified into:

- Training your brain to use divergent thinking.

- Then dividing large problems into smaller units to find a solution, or a new perspective by zooming out from the whole.

- Diving into the unknown to step outside of your comfort zone and create something fresh and new.

Look at me implementing divergent thinking. I'm actively splitting up these big ideas into more generalized ones to efficiently compare and contrast a computer scientist's creative process with that of an editorial photographer.

In the next and final part of this chapter, I outline the creative work of photographer Corey Bao Nguyen and contrast Kiara's simplified process against his.

It's funny because I also became friends with Corey in the strangest way. Apologies for sounding like a broken radio, but here it is again: life has its unusual ways of delivering lessons and placing meaningful people into your lives. And warning, this won't be the last time I reiterate this statement.

COREY BAO NGUYEN: THE RAW PHOTOGRAPHER

It was a Thursday morning, and I thought I would find some thrill in skipping all my classes and hitting Santa Monica Beach. I was right. The weather was a little uncomfortable, hot enough to roam around on the streets but a little brisk in the wind of the beach (maybe it was cold because it was the first time in a long time my hair was short).

While my suitemates and I were rolling around in the sand, our lips dripping with strawberries, we decided we wanted a monumental picture of us at the beach. So I grabbed my phone and tapped on the nearest person's shoulder.

It was Corey.

It's strange to look back at that moment. Back then, I wouldn't have guessed that I would be writing a book a year later and have Corey feature in it. When Corey was taking our pictures with my phone, he also took some sneaky selfies of himself.

Later, I posted the pictures on Instagram, and I decided to include Corey's selfie. Somehow within the magical web of the Internet someone found my profile, found his picture, and left a comment of Corey's Instagram handle, @bao.ii.

How did they find my profile, and how did they connect it to Corey's? Even after sixteen months, neither of us has a clue how that played out. The Internet is a simultaneously weird and beautiful place. Once we started texting, Corey and I were surprised to find out that we both were artists in our own right.

Corey is a Vietnamese photographer who lives in Dallas, Texas. All his photographs have a similar wash of minimalism and raw emotion. I was lucky enough to be able to stay in contact with Corey for a year and a half. It's strange to be able to stay in contact with basically a stranger from a different state, living a different life.

I gave him a call and asked if he would be interested in being interviewed for my book. When I asked him how he sees the world, he replied, "I gravitate toward the people; I think diversity is beautiful. What makes the world what it is today is the people; everything that happens on this Earth is from people." It warmed me to hear his response, and know there are other individuals who are just as enthralled as I am with humankind.

He started to fall in love with his camera and photography in 2014. At the time, his best friend had just lost his girlfriend in a car accident. Corey saw the shift of energy in his friend and wanted to embody that moment. He resolved to capture him in this moment of hurt, loss, and remorse.

Corey also wanted to make sure he told his best friend's story with as much purity and honesty as he could. All Corey had at the time was his GoPro, but despite the unconventional use of that device, he was able to feel the emotions from the images. Moreover, it allowed his best friend to open up. From that day on, every time Corey shoots, he treats it with the same respectful approach.

It is hard to present hurtful truth in a beautiful light. As an artist, you never want to diminish the feeling or take the story away from anyone. Instead, you want to show the beauty of those feelings because they are so utterly human. We are not entirely reasoned and reasonable creatures. We feel what we feel, no matter how irrational those feelings may be.

Corey's story conveys just that.

We shouldn't hide or shy away from hard emotions; we should be able to embrace being misunderstood and lost. We both agreed that the world is seen more beautifully through art, through being able to accept realities that may be painful—to sort through the thoughts that come with "fragile" stickers. This is Corey's way of implementing Kiara the computer scientist's idea of diving into the unknown to seek new perspectives. The unknown is a space that is inevitably uncomfortable and unfamiliar; these perplexing emotions that every human has, are in a way, an unfamiliar space.

Through art, Corey "notices more detail in people physically, things [he] wouldn't have noticed before." In the realm of art, there are no absolute rights and wrongs—only feelings that point in different directions. Because of the objective slate that art offers, Corey is able to notice more details.

Corey discussed with me the domino effect of letting art dim down his subjectivity and open up different sensory facets. Listening to a favorite song for the fifty-seventh time elicits the ability to hear a new sound, like a previously unnoticed layer of trumpets intertwining with violins. Corey points out that this way you no longer hear the song through the same constrained and limiting parameters.

Corey's creative process involves a lot of thinking and preparation. Again, with trying to paint any story with justice, it's essential to weigh all the perspectives.

In photography, he usually studies pictures of his subject and analyzes which features he wants to accentuate most. He imbues with his art with meaning, making sure to capture a *feeling*, not just eye-candy. Another vital part of his creative process is mentally preparing himself. To achieve this, Corey reminds himself to be receptive to all moods, atmospheres, and emotions. When he actively does this, he is able to connect with his subject and to have critical conversations with them. This allows his subsequent photography to be shaped around those conversations.

What's more real than capturing the topics you talk about when facing the pressure of a camera?

In this step of his creative process, Corey makes sure he zooms in on the bigger picture to look at the details of his subjects and shooting locations, in order to fully understand his parameters and fuel new perspectives and angles for his camera. This step can be compared to Kiara's second method of training her brain to use divergent thinking. In a similar way, Corey and Kiara both break apart larger ideas and concepts into minute components to find new "solutions" and perspectives. While Kiara implements this when solving complex algorithms, Corey does when seeking a fresh new way to present his subjects.

Lastly, for Corey, his creative process is also about connection. For him, this means having those critical conversations with subjects themselves and allowing the photography to be shaped around those conversations.

Even though Kiara Tanojo is a computer scientist and Corey Nguyen is a photographer, they both use the concepts of divergent thinking and seek the unknown to fuel their creativity.

WHAT THEY ALL HAVE IN COMMON: THE UCP

"In brief, CREATIVITY doesn't come free. It is not a gift or quirk of birth. Some people don't 'just have it' while others do not. Nor does it come from luck or magic. Creativity is learnable behavior requiring steady and determined effort."[51]

This quote comes from Don Koberg and Jim Bagnall's book *The All New Universal Traveler: A Soft-Systems Guide to Creativity, Problem-Solving, and the Process of Reaching Goals* in which their Universal Creative Process is outlined to tie all creators together.

Coincidentally, all four of these interviewees utilize the Universal Creative Process (UCP) in their own ways without realizing. Their loosely defined structure of what creativity means is a slight reflection of the UCP. In brief terms, UCP is a toolset that allows innovators of all kinds to develop creatively.

When introducing the framework, the authors first explain, "Gym teachers and geologists, writers and truck farmers, movie makers and motorcyclists, audiophiles and elevator operators, xylophonists and sci-fi fans are all problem-solvers."[52] While they may not realize, they all use creativity to overcome their everyday obstacles. The authors explain that the system was created by enmeshing problem solving processes from works as wide-ranging as Graham Wallas's 1926 model of creativity to the Osborn-Parnes creative problem solving procedure.[53]

---

51   Don Koberg and Jim Bagnall, *The All New Universal Traveler: A Soft-Systems Guide to Creativity, Problem-Solving, and the Process of Reaching Goals* (Crisp Publications, 1990), 9.

52   Don Koberg and Jim Bagnall, *The All New Universal Traveler: A Soft-Systems Guide to Creativity, Problem-Solving, and the Process of Reaching Goals* (Crisp Publications, 1990), 16.

53   Ibid.

The seven stages of the UCP that are outlined in the book (and that I have reinterpreted for myself) are:

1. Accept—Accepting a problem that exists has to be annoying enough for you to want to fix it.

2. Analyze—The research phase is understanding what works and what doesn't.

3. Define—Identify what the real problem is. Too often we are unsure of the specifics of why the mechanisms don't work.

4. Ideate—Divergent thinking should include weird, wacky ideas as the seeds of new innovation.

5. Select—Out of all your ideas, choose the most solid options; do a preliminary round of testing to see what choice seems attractive.

6. Implement—Carry out and pursue the strongest option (CAUTION: you most probably have to bounce back and forth on any of these steps to really know your strongest option.)

7. Evaluate—Show others your solution to evaluate both the problem and the solution again. You are never finished; this is the time to iterate.[54]

---

54 Don Koberg and Jim Bagnall, *The All New Universal Traveler: A Soft-Systems Guide to Creativity, Problem-Solving, and the Process of Reaching Goals* (Crisp Publications, 1990), 17.

Now that we've outlined The Universal Creative Process, let's project it back onto how these two photographers and engineers experience creative work.

We'll start with our Meticulous Engineer, Najwa Bou-Mel-hem. She analyzes the physical laws she's learned, to solve within the constraints of the problem. In one sentence, she has described steps one through three of the UCP.

Accepting and Analyzing the situation involves understanding the parameters of the problem. Defining is associated with immersing yourself in specialized knowledge to re-understand the problem.

Tim Tan, the Eccentric Photographer, has embraced step four: Ideating. We know that he's always had an eccentric way of creating, even at a young age, by refusing to follow the LEGOs instructions.

His idea of thinking outside of the box, yet realizing that there shouldn't have been a box to begin with, is the perfect mindset for Ideation. If you feel one hundred percent comfortable with your idea, chances are it's already out there and someone else has already enacted it.

Kiara Tanojo, the Empathic Computer Scientist, explains that some specific algorithms solve the same problems, but are executed in various ways. This part of her creative process coincides with steps five and six of the UCP.

While she is trying to think of novel solutions, she is essentially bouncing back and forth from Selection and Implementation. This search doesn't come naturally; you have to carry out different ideas through trial and error to see what works best.

Finally, Corey Nguyen, The Raw Photographer, represents the concluding key of the UCP. As we recently learned, Corey is able to see more details in people after he completes a study and photographs them. This is an important realization for step seven of the UCP: Evaluation.

Corey is able to see these additional details while he evaluates his "completed" creations. Despite his completion, Corey knows, each is only the beginning of future iterations. More ideas, details, and nuances will be brought to light during the Evaluation step, which is why, iterations will never end—you just decide when it's time to stop.

CHAPTER WRAP UP

- Creativity is not a linear process, and because of that it's not always comfortable.

    - Facing our fears and diving into the unknown are important facets to developing your creative process.

        - Learning and growth is found in these hard, uncomfortable spaces.

- There is creativity found in mechanical engineering and photography.

    - The simplified creative process of Najwa-Bou Melhem, the mechanical engineer, is:

        - Being exposed to the specific field.

- Combining her knowledge and inventiveness to develop a solution.

    - Thinking outside of the box for extra value.

  - These components are then re-illustrated throughout Tim Tan, the photographer's creative process—in a completely different way.

  - Tim's work can be found on Instagram at @perspec-gifs and @imtimtan.

- There is also creativity in computer science and editorial photography.

  - Computer scientist Kiara Tanojo's creative process requires training her brain, which involves:

    - Divergent thinking.

    - Diving into the unknown.

  - These two facets of thinking in different ways to promote creativity are also seen in the editorial photographer Corey Nguyen's process.

  - Corey's work can be found here, https://www.bao-ii.com/

- The above comparisons are illustrated to prove that the *only* difference between two career paths is medium, not level of creativity.

- The Universal Creative Process allows us to understand that creativity exists within all. We all use these processes, big and small, even to navigate our everyday problems.

- Finally, the diverse cultural background of all the interviewees inherently affects their creative work and understandings of the world.

  - This allows for the creative presentation of extremely varied perspectives.

5 + CONCLUSION

INCOMPARABLE NARRATIVES

Age as a Storyline

A middle-aged woman takes a sip of cheap vodka
and passes the flask around
allowing the liquid to swim in her bloodstream
the world begins to dance before their eyes
being drunk out of their minds, they try to sing
the alphabet backward,
attempting to harmonize each other
although they are forty-five years old, they are
intoxicated
unaware and
sixteen
again

A mother of two twins working two shifts at the
bank lives her life in haste

Instead of looking at the pedestrian light to signal
her when to walk
she looks up toward the stoplight
knowing that the green shifts to red faster,
giving her three extra seconds to cross the road
But today she waits
she messily paints her toenails a Hello Kitty pink
sipping on apple juice and living in slow motion
Today she is six
contented and
carefree

A man who inherits a mansion constructed by
Hephaestus himself
has a master's degree in biomedical engineering
from Harvard—
Rich enough to have 74 pairs of crocodile skin
loafers
and butlers in suits running around the house
Yesterday the whites of his eyes were a
constellation of red veins,
cheeks almost indented from constant drips
and drops.
Between uneven breaths
and blurred vision from the thick film of tears
He was two,
tantrums and
uncontrollable emotions.

—Sam Budiartho

OUR UNIQUE NARRATIVES:
THE BLUEPRINTS OF CREATIVITY

The poem above showcases that throughout someone's life, there are some days where we act five, or sixteen, or twenty-one. We've collated our life experiences at different ages and live through those different phases time and again.

As mentioned previously, creativity is the intersection of knowledge and imagination. While it is essential to have a vast imagination, to fuel innovative thinking, the facet of knowledge is equally as important. How could you continue to create without knowing the inner workings of your subject?

All the skills we've picked up in our younger selves seem like a distant memory but are usually reiterated in our older selves, consciously or subconsciously. As we grow, we develop our personal version of what creativity means and how to utilize it in our waking lives.

Our lives are not developed through a linear narrative. So, we must embrace the squiggly, jagged lines of our narratives because no two life experiences will ever be identical.

In the introduction of the book, I mentioned how all of us are walking stocks of information; we are databases of x years of living. Not one second of my life will ever be the same as the same second experienced by another person. I never really looked at people in such a manner until I met Derek Garlington. Derek is from New York and is a graduate student at the University of Southern California for screenwriting. He is the only member of his family that didn't go into psychology, but rather, chose to observe human psychology through a narrative lens. He is passionate about storytelling, which is why he's always thought of individuals in this way. He believes that people are full of stories and life lessons to be turned into a film for the viewers to then learn from.

Meeting people in unconventional ways seems to be a theme throughout this book. Derek and I met because we were both cast for one of the episodes of *Dr. Phil*.

It felt like a fever dream; I couldn't merely believe that I was at Paramount Studios for *Dr. Phil*. I was invited on the show through my Race and History of Los Angeles university class to be a part of the "Deconstructing Privilege" episode, which was aired on the CBS channel in October 2018. In the episode, varied individuals participated in a privilege walk. The show's host said statements and we either walked forward or backward one step, depending on whether we felt we had that privilege or not. For example, the host would say, "Step backward if you worry about walking home alone late at night" (unsurprisingly, all the women took a step backward for that one.)

Before any of the cast members set foot on stage, they had to go through hair and makeup. It made me feel oddly special to sit on one of those actor chairs, while fifty different people touched my face and hair. In the midst of applying makeup, Derek and I started talking to each other, asking one another how we got this crazy opportunity.

HOW SERENDIPITY WORKS

There seems to be a trend here. Looks like serendipity is leading me through my journey when meeting people. In a sense, it follows everyone if you pay enough attention.

Although, of course, serendipity can't do all that if you aren't receptive and open to others. Cuddling up to social connections (figuratively, unless you know the person really well) has its perks; it provides precious lessons. Human connection, knowledge, and creativity are intertwined concepts. Be open to these seemingly insignificant moments of connection—you never know how they might serve to benefit you.

A year and a half after *Dr. Phil*, Derek and I reached out to each other around the same time—asking for similar things.

When I asked Derek if I could interview him for a book on unlearning creativity, he asked if he could interview me for his documentary on creative processes. We were both tackling similar questions and concepts; the only difference was the medium—while I wrote the answers down, he filmed them. Fueled by his passion for documentaries, Derek has conducted many interviews. This was when I realized that I could analyze the creative process he's developed for filming his subjects while *he* was interviewing *me*.

CREATIVITY IN EVERYDAY CHALLENGES

When Derek set up his cameras and microphone, he noticed a low hum in the room: my fridge. While it may not seem like a big issue, it became one when his microphone couldn't capture clean and crisp audio of my answers. This problem allowed him to unintentionally showcase his creative problem-solving. He turned the fridge to the lowest setting, but also put his house keys inside to make sure we would remember to turn it back to its normal setting. It worked because when he was leaving, he checked for his house keys.

He then remembered to get them from the fridge and change the setting back to the coldest.

He developed this tactic early on while interviewing so many people in their homes. I guess when warm milk could be a direct consequence, the stakes become higher in remembering to turn the fridge back on.

IMAGINATION AS A CAREER

Once he finished filming me, I began interviewing him. I found out that Derek fell in love with art while going on long road trips. When he was a kid in the passenger seat of a driving car, he would imagine characters. He'd visualize cartoon characters jumping across buildings, skating across power lines, or on the road weaving between cars.

He would visualize that they were riding along with him. At that age, he didn't realize that imagining these figures would be vital to his much later creative process for screenwriting. When they were younger, Derek's cousin would belittle his creative process, saying, "you can't have imaginary friends. You're too old for that shit." In turn, Derek would be upset and stray away from verbalizing the scenes playing in his head during road trips.

Today, Derek knows that those very imaginary friends are part of the stories he tells now as a screenwriter. He would have these elaborate backstories for no reason, and although it was just his favorite childhood pastime, it turned into his career. Now, he allows himself to tap back into when he was five, seven, or ten years old, reimagining the narratives his brain developed when he was younger.

As a result, he ties all his experiences and imaginary friends into his passion: commentary toward the greater good.

At a point in his life, Derek questioned whether he should be a filmmaker. He wanted to bring change but realized that his passion didn't involve something like heart surgery. Derek wondered about the importance of films. Why do we need new movies? There are so many films already, of all different genres, illustrating a vast amount of narratives—so why do we still need more?

As he's grown, he realized that there's an endless desire for humans to create and be creative, in all forms—from developing vaccines to designing rain boots—because the world itself is always changing. Within this ever-changing world, films often offer us context for and catharsis from current societal norms; narratives usually have some sort commentary or connection to the here and now.

Derek realizes now that even though he's not bringing change through heart surgery, he is still contributing to meaningful change. Through screenwriting he has the potential to educate the masses via compelling narratives.

Regarding new perspectives built from other people's narratives, Derek says, "I think [different narratives] allows us, in a very human way, to see [what] affect[s] us in ways we may not even realize." In this context, it is equally important to realize that everyone is a storyteller in their own mode. For example, the way an architect tells their story is through meticulous blueprints and measurements.

A large portion of life revolves around stories. Derek explains that "people always say they have a bad memory, but if you want to remember specific things, putting them into a story setting, even if it's just a grocery list, embeds it better. So I think that tells us something about our innate human nature, that we crave storytelling."

We're *all* storytellers, who simultaneously seek stories from other storytellers—whether it's through painting, technology, psychology, or coding. Innately, as storytellers, we can teach and learn from others. Our world is *this* advanced because of the billions upon billions upon billions of different narratives it holds. Individuals and groups can invent innovation after innovation because of their knowledge and imagination—their creative thinking. Society, and the individuals within it, are often inspired by stories that drive scientific advancement.

Unfortunately, only a particular set of individuals believe they are creative—and the rest don't. It becomes an "us" and "them" situation. We are taught these sharp divisions through institutional reinforcement and believe in them, starting from a young age. We learn that to be creative, we must have these specific narratives—how to think or what professions to pursue—but all that goes against the point of being creative.

We are creative because we have diverse narratives.

Perhaps the best way that creativity works in today's age is through learning how to unlearn it. To understand the constraints of creativity that society has developed, and to break it apart. To also understand that creativity cannot be taught, but rather can only be expanded through experience.

The context and environment of the word "creativity" are in desperate need of a paradigm shift.

THE KUHN CYCLE: PARADIGM SHIFT

An effective way of explaining the creation of knowledge and beliefs is the Kuhn Cycle. Our belief systems are continually changing and breaking. The Kuhn Cycle was initially introduced by Thomas Kuhn in 1962, in his work called "The Structure of Scientific Revolutions." Kuhn developed the Cycle to challenge his contemporary world's perception of science.[55]

The Cycle starts with a paradigm: a model that fits all our pre-existing beliefs about the world. The next stage of the Cycle is a new discovery that *doesn't* fit into the boundaries of the paradigm. When new observations are found to be an anomaly and are unable to fit into the existing paradigm, it creates a model crisis. This new model crisis then destroys the old paradigm to create a broader, more inclusive model that incorporates the added knowledge.[56]

The Cycle repeats itself when new knowledge that doesn't fit the currently existing paradigm is found.[57] And so on, and so on.

---

55   "The Kuhn Cycle," Thwink.org, accessed May 3, 2020.

56   Ibid.

57   Ibid.

An article posted in the *British Journal of Sports Medicine*, written by Flávio de Oliveira Pires, breaks down Thomas Kuhn's "Cycle of Scientific Revolutions." de Oliveira Pires explains that "the Kuhnian model argues that science does not progress through slow acceleration of data but in revolutions," since any scientific progress can be distinguished through the paradigm cycle.[58]

When new information is discovered, "anomalies may accumulate and create a 'crisis' which approaches a scientific revolution," thus forcing society to redefine prior knowledge.[59]

The paradigm our society currently holds for the concept of creativity is outdated. A bigger, bolder, more inclusive definition is needed to fully encapsulate the definition of creativity and to destroy the constrictions we've learned about it. We must, crucially, also break the cycle of labeling only a certain set of individuals as creative.

The new paradigm of creativity should be inclusive of everyone, recognizing that each unique narrative serves as the backbone of our creative forces.

THE FULL RECAP
We are encouraged to think outside of the box but within still more parameters. We often overlook the idea that creativity

---

58 Flávio de Oliveira Pires, "Thomas Kuhn's 'Structure of Scientific Revolutions' Applied to Exercise Science Paradigm Shifts: Example Including the Central Governor Model," *British Journal of Sports Medicine* 47, no. 11 (July 19, 2013): 721.

59 Ibid.

cannot be taught and that learning it is not a linear process. Everyone navigates and curates their creative process at their own pace and manner.

At a young age, students and individuals are taught the definition of creativity as artsy, as musical notes, paint strokes on a canvas, or rhyming couplets, but never chemicals in beakers, worksheets full of numbers, or parts of a motherboard. This socially defined concept of creativity is misleading; it highlights only those individuals who write in verse, but never those who write in code.

Because of this, many of us who do not dabble in traditional art may start to project statements such as, "I'm just not the creative type." Many constantly downplay their creative thinking processes, which in turn hinders their inventive powers. It's a self-fulfilling prophecy.

To me, the definition of creativity is finding unique solutions to problems—no matter how complicated or elementary the situation. Finding these creative solutions is only possible through the intersection of knowledge, personal experiences, and imagination.

To expand our knowledge as a tool for creativity, we must be receptive to human connection. Our connections allow us to view the world in a multitude of ways, which provides important lessons. We've all grown up starring in different narratives; what better way to learn than to hear from other stars?

Again, I fit perfectly into the current frame of what is deemed as creative because I spend a lot of time developing two-dimensional art and design. But when I started comparing my strengths with those of non-traditional artists, I realized that the difference between our career paths is not creativity, but rather medium.

From an overarching standpoint, all the interviewees I've showcased are pursuing such contrasting career paths and come from a diverse set of cultural backgrounds. They all grew up in different parts of the world and are by nature and nurture inclined to think and see in divergent ways.

What all of these individuals have in common is their creativity, and that we all met in such unconventional ways. These stories, I hope, reiterate the importance of being receptive to social connection.

So, can *everyone* be a creative? Let's review the evidence.

In the introduction of the book, we met Jeanette the Uber driver. From her, we learned that creativity is not limited to a specific type of person, but can be found in everyone through the way they problem-solve. The universe, after all, has exciting ways of showcasing lessons and integrating meaningful people into your lives.

This tied into Professor Matthew Liberman's study on how we have evolved to be extremely social animals—always pondering about social situations, even while our brains are at rest.

Human connection is an essential facet to learning; we are all databases of information and our experiences are unique from one person to another.

In chapter one of the book, we heard the two significant perspectives of creativity. While Ken Robinson's theory illustrates that unhindered imagination is vital to think of inventive solutions, Tim Leunig believes that it is knowledge that grounds creativity. For the purposes of this book I have proposed that creativity is not merely one or the other, but is rather the intersection of imagination and knowledge.

Although we need imagination to dream big and remove ourselves from the constraints of reality to find new solutions, we also need knowledge. Knowledge is the basis of understanding and of turning an imaginative solution into something real.

The subsequent section revolved around the left and right brain. The left hemisphere primarily works in the field of logic, analytical thinking, and language, while the right in emotion, creativity, and random thinking.

We then met a computer science undergraduate student named Alex Baker, who showcases an example of left-brain dominant problem-solving while debunking Grandma's escape room. During this experience, we saw the comparison between diverse strategic thinking via his left-brain dominance and my right-brain dominance.

While we each have our respective brain dominance, it is important to remember that both hemispheres work in coordination to fully function—proving that everyone is innately creative, but exemplifies it in different ways. The left-brain is important for Alex to analyze code, while the right is vital for the invention of his creative solutions.

We also learned in this chapter that, so far, scientists can't agree or disagree whether the left brain controls analytical thinking, and the right with visual thinking. Further research still needs to be done in understanding if split hemisphere functions are real.

This section of the book also held the first example of a non-traditional artist as creative. Even though Alex Baker is a computer science major, he has proven his creativity by using both knowledge and imagination to seek innovative coding (and escape room) solutions.

Besides logic, empathy is also a main driving factor of creativity. In the third chapter, devoted to my own creative process, we learned that everyone's creative process looks different. There is no singular way to take in and process information. It may be necessary to move away from how we were taught to learn, to find new thinking processes that resonate.

Creativity is used in more than just the act of drawing—it significantly involves how you pivot when hitting a dead end before overcoming that and more obstacles.

We are also introduced to Nisha Khater, the photographer I collaborated with for *To Build A Home.* Collaboration is critical in any learning environment; it allows for the opportunity of artistic generating from another perspective.

To enhance our creative endeavors, we must be open and receptive to our absurd thoughts and dreams—they are a rush of inspiration in disguise.

In the next segment, Jacan's notebook taught us to dive into the unknown and face our fears. As individuals, we have grown comfortable in sticking to routine and certainty. Fear and the unknown are two concepts that all of us are uncomfortable with, but growth is found in these uncomfortable spaces.

Within the sections of fear and the unknown, we compared and contrasted four individuals, two of which are traditional artists and photographers—Tim Tan and Corey Nguyen. The other two are non-traditional artists and engineers, Najwa Bou-Melhem and Kiara Tanojo.

When comparing these distinctive fields, we found that a lot of the concepts of creativity overlap from one field to another. Bottom line is: traditional and non-traditional artists use creativity to think ingeniously, no matter their career.

We then learned about the Universal Creative Process, which allows us to understand that creativity is used all the time, throughout every single person—even to weave through our everyday problems.

In this chapter, the final one, we are introduced to Derek Garlington, the screenwriter who made me believe that everyone has a unique narrative worth knowing. These narratives are built through personal experiences, which inevitably affect their creativity and how they choose which medium to showcase it.

To wrap everything with a neat and pretty bow, we then learned about the Kuhn cycle and that a creativity paradigm shift is needed because everyone should be viewed as a true creative.

PERSONAL REMARKS & A CALL TO ACTION

In writing this book I've not only grown as a writer, but also as an individual. It wasn't just putting words on the screen and calling it a day—it was also intensely frustrating, enticing, and personal. Even though some parts of the process were demanding and stressful, at the end of the day I always found a glimmer of realization, reminding me that this is a passion project. Throughout the writing process I let myself feel a range of emotions to make sure each string of words is honest as possible.

As a non-confrontational person, I've nevertheless had to confront my thoughts and the belief systems I grew to live by. While writing, I had to sit through my abstract ideas while analyzing myself, the people around me, and society as a whole, for months.

This has coincided with the COVID-19 pandemic. I admit, while combing through the chapters with global catastrophe on my mind, I questioned the worth and purpose of the book.

That said, everything in this book reflects my passion and what I believe is an essential part of the world: creativity and social connection. But why do I think these topics are so important?

When COVID-19 started, all of a sudden, individuals across the globe were separated—deprived of being able to see their loved ones. Random conversations with the people we encounter outside of our homes were significantly reduced. These nuances may have been taken for granted while they existed, but they are definitely longed for and often thought about now.

Before writing the book, I knew that humans were social animals, but I never got to see the true extent of this until I did the research and then witnessed how everyone is facing adverse side effects from social distancing. Writing this book in such a strange time has impacted my view on creativity and human connection, a lot more than I thought it would. As we all know very well at this point, the pandemic has shifted our understanding of normalcy by quite a lot.

To navigate this new way of living has involved *a lot* of creativity, and will continue to involve it moving forward. To make progress, new innovations and strategies are needed—and creativity is the key factor of it all.

The pandemic can be the chance to work on our creative processes. Creativity, in turn, can help integrate us into our new normal, and help reduce the great suffering across the globe. This information and these innovative strategies can then be passed down onto generations after generations, making sure our world is more prepared and advanced.

It only takes a shift in perspective to see the silver linings—the hard part is being open to that viewpoint.

I wrote this book because of all the people I've met who automatically claim they aren't a creative person. I grew tired of society sealing people off into predetermine boxes.

I wrote this book in hopes of contributing to a paradigm shift in the way we think about creative work. The first step of solving any problem, or initiating a paradigm shift, is recognition. This book encourages its readers to recognize that our definition of creativity is flawed.

We are a long way away from a true shift—it is a big task to actively change a long-ingrained belief. Before we try to change our perception as a society on creativity, we should start on a smaller scale.

Let's focus on what *you* can do:

- Face the unknown and embrace your specific way of understanding and creating.

- Remind others that they are creative, and explain to them why they are, if need be.

- Realize that creativity is already luxuriously living in your mind, rent free.

When we all actively do this, only then will the paradigm shift slowly follow.

APPENDIX

———

INTRODUCTION

Smith, Emily. "Social Connection Makes a Better Brain." *The Atlantic*. October 29, 2013.
https://www.theatlantic.com/health/archive/2013/10/social-connection-makes-a-better-brain/280934/

CHAPTER 1

Robinson, Ken. "Do schools kill creativity?" Filmed February 2006 in Monterey, CA. TED video, 6:28.
https://www.ted.com/talks/sir_ken_robinson_do_schools_kill_creativity?language=en#t-1110

Robinson, Ken. "Do schools kill creativity?" February 2006 in Monterey, CA. TED video, 18:14.
https://www.ted.com/talks/sir_ken_robinson_do_schools_kill_creativity?language=en#t-1110

Robinson, Ken. *Out of Our Minds: Learning to be Creative*. Mankato: Capstone, 2011.

Sack, Harald. "Christopher Latham Sholes invented the QWERTY Typewriter." *SciHi Blog*. February 14, 2018.
http://scihi.org/christopher-latham-sholes-qwerty-typewriter/

Stevens, Susannah. "How this couch changed everything." *BBC*. June 18, 2015.
https://www.bbc.com/news/magazine-33079041

TED. "Tim Leunig: Why real creativity is based on knowledge." October 17, 2016. Video, 0:22.
https://www.youtube.com/watch?v=vajIsWwHEMc

TED. "Tim Leunig: Why real creativity is based on knowledge." October 17, 2016. Video, 2:35.
https://www.youtube.com/watch?v=vajIsWwHEMc

TED. "Tim Leunig: Why real creativity is based on knowledge." October 17, 2016. Video, 5:50.
https://www.youtube.com/watch?v=vajIsWwHEMc

CHAPTER 2

Carbon, Claus-Christian, and Sabine, Alberchet. "Bartlett's Schema Theory: the Unreplicated 'Portrait D'homme' Series from 1932." *Quarterly Journal of Experimental Psychology* 65, no. 11 (November 2012): 2258–70. doi:10.1080/17470218.2012.696121

Form, Sven, and Kaernbach, Christian. "More Is Not Always Better: The Differentiated Influence of Empathy on Different Magnitudes of Creativity." *Europe's Journal of Psychology*, vol. 14, 1 (March 2018): 54-65. https://www.ncbi.nlm.nih.gov/pmc/articles/PMC5973517/

Levine, Michael. "Logic and Emotion." *Psychology Today*. July 12, 2012. https://www.psychologytoday.com/sg/blog/the-divided-mind/201207/logic-and-emotion

Shmerling, Robert H. "Right brain/left brain, right?" Harvard Health Publishing. August 25, 2017, updated November 8, 2019. https://www.health.harvard.edu/blog/right-brainleft-brain-right-2017082512222

Smith, E.E. "Are You Left- or Right-Brain Dominant?" *Psychology Today*. October 19, 2012. https://www.psychologytoday.com/sg/blog/not-born-yesterday/201210/are-you-left-or-right-brain-dominant

Tapaniya, Dalsukh. "Colors in UI Design—Theory, Psychology & Practice." *Medium*. May 26, 2019. https://medium.com/iconscout/colors-in-ui-design-theory-psychology-practice-f6d6a5e6e04d

CHAPTER 3

Gross, Veronica. "Frequently Asked Questions about Synesthesia," *Boston University*. Accessed May 5, 2020. https://www.bu.edu/synesthesia/faq/

Johnson, Reed. "The Mystery of S., The Man with an Impossible Memory." *The New Yorker*. August 12, 2017. https://www.newyorker.com/books/page-turner/the-mystery-of-s-the-man-with-an-impossible-memory

Luria, A. R. *The Mind of a Mnemonist*. Cambridge: Harvard University Press, 1987.

NPR Staff. "Pharrell Williams on Juxtaposition and Seeing Sounds." *NPR*, December 31, 2013. https://www.npr.org/sections/therecord/2013/12/31/258406317/pharrell-williams-on-juxtaposition-and-seeing-sounds

CHAPTER 4

Encyclopaedia Britannica Online. Technology ed. s.v. "History of Photography." Accessed May 5, 2020. https://www.britannica.com/technology/photography/Development-of-stereoscopic-photography

Herbert, Frank. *Dune*. London: New English Library, 1972.

Koberg, Don, and Jim Bagnall. *The All New Universal Traveler: A Soft-Systems Guide to Creativity, Problem-Solving, and the Process of Reaching Goals.* Crisp Publications, 1990.

CONCLUSION & CHAPTER 5

Pires, Flávio de Oliveira. "Thomas Kuhn's 'Structure of Scientific Revolutions' Applied to Exercise Science Paradigm Shifts: Example Including the Central Governor Model." *British Journal of Sports Medicine* 47, no. 11 (July 19, 2013): 721. http://bjsm.bmj.com/content/47/11/721.full.pdf.

Thwink.org. "The Kuhn Cycle." Accessed May 3, 2020. https://www.thwink.org/sustain/glossary/KuhnCycle.htm

EXTRAS PAGE (PROMOTION):

———

If you're reading this, give yourself some love and juicy strawberries. Thank you for being here and spending some time with me.

If you enjoyed this book and would like to learn more about my art and myself, check these fun extensions out:

www.sambudiartho.com

www.instagram.com/sambudiarts

Made in the USA
Middletown, DE
17 August 2020

15110996R00089